EXTENDING YOUR CONGREGATION'S WELCOME: INTERNAL CLIMATE AND INTENTIONAL OUTREACH

W. James Cowell

DISCIPLESHIP RESOURCES

MATERIALS FOR GROWTH IN CHRISTIAN FAITH AND LIFE

P.O. Box 189 • Nashville, TN 37202 • Phone (615) 340-7285

ACKNOWLEDGMENTS

For several years I have been a part of a team of persons from the Section on Evangelism, General Board of Discipleship, The United Methodist Church, that has led an emphasis on "Offering Christ Today" across the country. Part of my responsibility in those schools has been to challenge persons to evaluate the spiritual climate of their congregation and to consider more intentional outreach efforts. My task has been to provide "handles" to approach these subjects. This book is a result of those presentations.

I am indebted to lay persons and clergy in many denominations who have shared ideas and programs that are working in their churches. Many of those ideas are included in this book. I am also indebted to the congregations I have served in Tennessee, Kentucky, and Colorado for the insights in ministry which they have communicated to me. Without apology I refer to experience gleaned from those rich and rewarding years of pastoral ministry.

Special thanks go to my colleagues, the staff of the Section on Evangelism: Suzanne G. Braden, Sang E. Chun, Shirley F. Clement, H. Eddie Fox, Joe A. Harding, David W. Kerr, and Rodney T. Smothers (now pastor at Central United Methodist Church, Atlanta, Georgia). In their own way, they have contributed to this book.

Grateful appreciation is due Prestine Carter and Jane Massey for their able assistance in the preparation of this manuscript. My wife, Norma, has talked over many of these ideas with me, and I acknowledge her continued support.

Library of Congress Catalog Card No. 88-83992

ISBN 0-88177-068-X

DR068B

CONTENTS

FOREWORD

Evangelism is rooted in the nature of God revealed in Jesus Christ. God is a pursuing, seeking, and persisting God who constantly and consistently reaches out to humanity.

The Christian congregation is a primary instrument of this evangelization. A congregation does not have a program of evangelism; it is the vehicle of evangelizing. This book puts the emphasis in the key place of the congregation. The congregation must intentionally and aggressively reach out with the good news of Jesus Christ and welcome all people into this fellowship. This book is designed to help a congregation develop life and ministry of intentional outreach.

I know of no one more qualified to write this book than Jim Cowell. He has distinguished himself as a pastor, minister of evangelism in a mega-church, a new church pastor, and as a national leader in evangelism. He is sensitive and open to discovering new ways for the congregation to be faithful to the evangelistic mandate.

Jim has visited hundreds of congregations, and he has gathered in this book hundreds of ideas which can help your congregation. He has uncovered many matters which are as vital as the bones and flesh are in the life of a person. Through these vital structures moves the Spirit which gives the congregation life. This book is solidly grounded in biblical foundation.

There are ideas galore in the following pages for every size congregation. I pray that, as you read it, you will be inspired to be a faithful congregation which evangelizes the good news of Jesus Christ.

H. Eddie Fox
World Director of Evangelism
World Methodist Council

INTRODUCTION

What is our purpose in and through the congregation? Are we aware of our mission?

While leading a church workshop in Las Vegas, I visited the Tropicana Hotel for lunch. On the wall opposite the administrative offices of the hotel was this posted statement:

> **Tropicana Mission Statement**
> The Tropicana Resort and Casino is in the business of offering various forms of quality entertainment in a gaming environment to its customers so as to maximize long-term profitability for its shareholders. To accomplish this the Tropicana is committed to constantly attracting new customers and building a broad base of contented repeat guests who are served by a staff of dedicated, satisfied, customer-oriented employees.
> —*Ramada Renaissance Resort and Casino*

At least the resort and casino management knew what they were seeking to accomplish. Is it as clear to us, as Christian congregations, that we are to be about the task of making disciples of Jesus Christ?

This book looks at the climate of a congregation and its intentional outreach—two sides of the same coin. To make disciples we must reach out to persons as they are, but we must also have a welcoming, receiving, hospitable community of faith into which to incorporate those persons. Thus, Parts I and II of this book seek to help congregations assess their interior life in order to reach out more effectively.

No book can exhaust the subject of the climate or outreach of a congregation. Through questions and illustrations, this resource suggests how a church might improve its welcoming posture and extended fellowship. Concrete "handles" are given, not to be copied necessarily but to stimulate one's imagination about what might work in his/her own context and congregation. Those ideas might provoke further exploration of new directions to take in future planning at your church.

Many denominations or congregations have embarked on campaigns to increase church attendance. I affirm and appreciate these marketing efforts and attempts to raise the visibility of a denomination and local congregations. Yet, I would like to think that something significant happens to individuals who see billboards or bumper stickers or other media advertisements and actually come to a church to "check out the action," spiritually speaking.

An admonition is often found above church nurseries: "We shall not all sleep, but we shall all be changed" (1 Corinthians 15:51-52, RSV). May something written here be the stimulus for positive change in your congregation as you faithfully seek to make disciples.

Part One:
Creating a Climate of Hospitality

I. A Positive Congregational Climate

"**P**ut your best foot forward. You never have a second chance to make a first impression." Usually, these words are uttered to a friend or relative preparing for a job interview. You should not be surprised to know that the statements also hold true for a local congregation of Christian people. Congregations make initial and lasting impressions on people, especially first-time visitors. In talking about the reasons churches grow, nothing can replace the welcoming posture of a congregation toward visitors.

As a new church pastor in Colorado Springs, I went to visit a couple who attended our Sunday worship service. They had recently moved to Colorado Springs from the Denver area. They had joined a small church on the outskirts of that great city because they wished to be a part of a church in their neighborhood. Several weeks after they joined, they entered the church on Sunday for the worship service and started to sit down. However, a shrill voice declared, "That's my pew." Though the couple moved to another pew in the sanctuary, they never returned to that church. They became inactive members.

Friends of ours had a similar experience when they visited the church we attend on Sunday morning. The husband let his wife and children out of the car at the sanctuary door, saying he would join them after parking the car. The wife and children were seated near the front of the sanctuary by an usher. By the time the husband joined them, the sanctuary was becoming quite crowded. As he attempted to join the rest of his family on a pew, an elderly person sitting on the same pew remarked, "Where do you think you're going to sit, sonny?" Since this member would not relinquish her seat to visitors, the visiting wife put hymnals on both sides of a wooden divider in the pew and sat on that divider for the entire service. The family did not join our church!

On the other hand, some congregations convey a spirit of

3

warmth and acceptance to persons who attend the Sunday worship services. Dr. Norman Neaves, pastor of the Church of the Servant in Oklahoma City, shared the following letter in the church's newsletter:

> It probably doesn't mean that much to you or to the others in your church, but one of the most important things of all (in your service on Sunday morning) to me is when we hold hands to sing the Lord's Prayer. I live alone. I am also without a job now and I don't have any friends. I guess you would say I'm very shy and I am. I've never been very good at relating to people. . . .
>
> This might be difficult for you to believe, Norman. But each Sunday morning when I hold hands with the people near me and we sing the Lord's Prayer, it is the only time during the week that somebody touches me and I touch somebody. Little touches have become so important. Touching the hand of a clerk upon exchanging money, pressing my shoulder against another person in the elevator at the hospital the other day, these are so important to me because they make me feel connected just a bit. But nothing is so special as to feel the warmth from another person's hand when we sit together and sing.
>
> I hope you won't quit doing that on Sunday morning. It's such a little thing, I know, but believe me it means so much to me. I need to be touched, I want to be touched, I want to reach out and touch, but sometimes it's just very hard for me to do. I hope you will understand.[1]
>
> —(Name withheld)

II. What Is Climate?

Climate relates to the overall presence that a congregation shares and conveys to visitors. Perhaps one of the best definitions of climate is given by Ben Johnson in *An Evangelism Primer: Practical Principles for Congregations:* "Climate in a church resists definition, but even untrained visitors recognize it. In fact, it speaks *first* and *loudest* to every visitor who enters the service of worship. Climate is that 'sense' or 'spirit' of a congregation. It includes the members' relation to Christ, to each other, to new persons, their attitude toward change, the future and the growth of the church. These complex attitudes and relationships, plus the presence of 'the Holy,' combine to create the climate of a congregation."[2]

If a congregation says it wants to grow but the wrong climate or the wrong spiritual atmospheric conditions are present, that church faces an impossible task. Herb Miller, a church growth consultant, offers an impressive image: "If the wrong climate inhabits a congregation, introducing better methods succeeds like hailstones against a Sherman tank."[3] His own experience validates the fact that "the world's worst air pollution is the negative smog found in some congregations."[4]

Assessing the climate for growth and evangelization is essential if congregations are ever to reach out and claim the future and other persons for Christ's sake. The continued membership loss of many mainline denominations over the last two decades has created much analysis and discussion about the causes of decline. Sometimes denominational membership goals are established to spur churches to reverse the decline.

Increasingly, officials of many denominations are recognizing a spiritual malaise or sense of apathy that has gripped many congregations. That questioning of a church's purpose and ability to receive newcomers is also reflected in the attitude of unchurched persons in the 1988 study of *The Unchurched American* conducted by the Gallup Organization, Inc.

> Issues on which there is significant disagreement among the churched and unchurched include whether or not churches and synagogues today:
> • Have a clear sense of the real spiritual nature of religion
> • Are effective in helping people find the meaning of life
> • Are accepting of outsiders
> • Are too restrictive in their preachings about morality
> • Are concerned too much with organizational issues and not enough about social justice
> Clearly the unchurched take a more negative view of the church when it comes to these matters.[5]

It is unlikely that a congregation will be effective in reaching out to others if a sense of indifference or the wrong spiritual climate persists! Corrective measures start by, first, looking inward. As one editorial stated:

> Those of us who are now members need to attend to our own spiritual health before we can effectively lead others into the church.
> Among other things, we need to find and practice ways of experiencing and responding to the life-transforming grace of God in our lives, both individually and collectively. . . . Unless we are living examples of the good news we proclaim—and openly acknowledge our ultimate dependence upon the grace of God—it is highly improbable that we can persuade . . . other spiritually needy people that our church is "where the action is."[6]

Growth does not come easily. Reversing trends within any local congregation calls for intentionality and perseverance. Yet, we who believe in a God who can change lives, also believe that same God can assist persons in reshaping the future of congregations.

Almost any church can grow, numerically as well as spiritually, if great effort is expended, along with an ultimate reliance upon God's guiding presence to actually bring results in terms of spirituality or numbers. It is God who builds up God's church. (See Matthew 16:18.) We are faithful to a task, but God gives the increase!

I learned of one church in Kentucky that had a membership of one (that's right, *one*). The annual conference had not officially closed the church. The one member wanted that church to continue its long history and heritage. Then a student pastor was appointed to the three-point circuit that included this church of one member. Soon he was visiting in the community, seeking persons to be a part of that church. People responded to his visits and concern and began to attend and even offered to help fix up the physical facility where the people gathered. Persons in the community soon learned when the pastor would be out of classes and visiting in the community, so they prepared meals to "tide him over." It was not long until that church of *one* member had an average attendance of *nine!* A pastor and one lay person wanted that church to serve its community, and great things happened.

III. Factors That Affect Congregational Climate

What are the factors that impact the spiritual climate within a congregation? John Ed Mathison, pastor at Frazer Memorial United Methodist Church in Montgomery, Alabama, collected a list of contrasts between "live churches" and "dead churches." His list is as follows:

Live churches are planning for the future—
 Dead churches are reliving the past.
Live churches focus on people—
 Dead churches focus on programs—
Live churches present an unchanging Christ in forms of ministry that are changing—
 Dead churches do things the way they have always been done.
Live churches are filled with tithers—
 Dead churches are filled with tippers.
Live churches are friendly and receptive to newcomers—
 Dead churches wonder why they have no visitors.
Live churches focus on what's right with the church—
 Dead churches look for what's wrong with the church.
Live churches design worship in which the worshipers are participants—
 Dead churches have worshipers who are spectators.
Live churches have worship that celebrates—
 Dead churches have worship that is endured.
Live churches support missions heavily—
 Dead churches keep the money at home.
Live churches dream God's dreams—
 Dead churches relive nightmares.
Live churches have music designed for the congregation—
 Dead churches have music designed for the musician.
Live churches focus on power—
 Dead churches focus on problems.[7]

John Ed Mathison concluded this listing on the front of his church newsletter by saying: "See you at the 'live' place Sunday!"

It is no accident that Frazer Memorial is among the fastest growing (if not *the* fastest growing) United Methodist churches in the country. Dr. Mathison, author of *Every Member in Ministry* (available from Discipleship Resources), is quick to point out principles that support growth and apply to churches of any size.

Though the various factors are listed below separately, each of these factors is intermeshed with each other.

1. **The love and acceptance of the membership for each other.** An IBM ad for a computer product stated: "If user-friendly isn't friendly enough, try INTELLECT.* It's almost affectionate." The ad went on to state: "INTELLECT comes with a basic vocabulary that you can expand by including your own terms. If you use a word it doesn't yet understand, it politely asks you to confirm the spelling or supply another term. And it logs all unfamiliar terms to be included in the future."[8]

This ad demonstrates that in spite of advances in technology, there is still the need for the human touch. John Naisbitt, in his bestseller, *Megatrends,* included a chapter entitled "From Forced Technology to High Tech/High Touch." In that chapter Naisbitt writes:

> What happens is that whenever new technology is introduced into society, there must be a counterbalancing human response—that is, *high touch*—or the technology is rejected. The more high tech, the more high touch. . . .
>
> Now, at the dawn of the twenty-first century, high tech/high touch has truly come of age. Technology and our human potential are the two great challenges and adventures facing humankind today. The great lesson we must learn from the principle of high tech/high touch is a modern version of the ancient Greek ideal—*balance.*
>
> *We must learn to balance the material wonders of technology with the spiritual demands of our human nature.* [9]

Naisbitt is right. The need for "high touch" today is reflected in the needs of persons coming to our churches. The more impersonal a society becomes, the more personal our approach to persons must become so that each person can feel included in the fellowship of believers. "Passing the peace" becomes not only a nice addition to the order of service for some persons but a necessity— a symbol that one *belongs.*

The love and acceptance of the membership for each other is not determined by the size of the membership. In some small town churches, persons on the left of the center aisle hardly speak to persons on the right of the center aisle before or after the morning worship hour. On the other hand, churches with several thousand in attendance can communicate through touch and other means so that everyone is a brother and sister.

2. A contagious sense of expectancy. A conference of one denomination did a survey of twenty-five growing churches. Among the general characteristics of these churches, representing various size congregations within the conference, was "a contagious sense of expectancy." The conference report elaborated on this characteristic by explaining that "(a) the congregation has a good self-image, (b) there is joy in the life and work of the church, (c) there is a sense of the power of the gospel to change lives; confidence in the ability of *this* congregation to be an agent of that gospel, and (d) a desire to excel: to do better and better."[10] The opposite of a contagious sense of expectancy is a defeatist attitude.

A contagious sense of expectancy is rooted in a strong faith in God and an overwhelming sense of God's presence and power. Expectancy is not rooted in an unquestioning belief in human ingenuity. Congregations displaying this sense of expectancy are standing on tiptoe to see what God will do next, because the collective body of believers is attempting things that can be accomplished *only if God is a part of the plan.* Finite efforts are supplemented by spiritual power.

3. Trust between pastor and laity. A climate of trustworthiness means that lines of communication between clergy and laity are open and that proper channels are used in carrying ideas to fruition. A pastor of a growing church states: "There is no magic to trustworthiness. For church leaders, it means 'going by the book.' That means presenting proposals to the proper boards or committees before action has begun. It also means being willing to 'lose' graciously on an idea and not seek other means of implementing my plan. It means living by the budget and not seeking to get what I want by 'special gifts.'"[11] Succinctly, it means that the pastor will not make an "end run." It also means that laity will not try to "slip one by" the pastor by calling home meetings or committee meetings without the pastor's knowledge. Trust works both ways.

It is hard for pastors to see dreams defeated by the vote of an Administrative Board or Council. To carry out dreams means attitudes must be changed, priorities must be redirected, budgets must be redistributed. It does not happen overnight. Sometimes "opposition" forms against the very idea/program that the pastor feels would serve the community around the church. There is still the need for pastor and laity to discuss intelligently and act with integrity. When there is mutual trust and mutual ministry is being conducted through the church, newcomers soon become aware of it. When tension exists between clergy and laity within a congregation, that is also communicated and affects the climate of growth.

4. **The congregation's attitude toward change.** The story is told of a man who arrived late for a board meeting at the church. Someone had brought up the need for a new chandelier in the sanctuary to add more light to the area. The latecomer caught the tail end of the discussion and rose to his feet to announce, "I'm against it." He proceeded to give his reasons. "It costs too much. We don't have anyone who can play it. What we really need is more light." Sometimes persons are quick to judge an idea before they have adequate information to make an informed decision.

Change does not come easy for some people. A parable about a lobster illustrates the problem which many people have in breaking out of the "ruts" of living.

> Long ago, when the world was very new . . . there was a certain lobster who determined that the Creator had made a mistake. So he set up an appointment to discuss the matter. "With all due respect," said the lobster, "I wish to complain about the way you designed my shell. You see, I just get used to one outer casing, when I've got to shed it for another. Very inconvenient and rather a waste of time."
>
> To which the Creator replied, "I see. But do you realize that it is the giving up of one shell that allows you to grow into another?"
>
> "But I like myself just the way I am," the lobster said.
>
> "Your mind's made up?" the Creator asked.
>
> "Indeed!" the lobster stated firmly.
>
> "Very well," smiled the Creator. "From now on, your shell will not change . . . and you may go about your business just as you are right now."
>
> "That's very kind of you," said the lobster, and left.
>
> At first, the lobster was very content with wearing the same old shell. But as time passed, he found that his once light and comfortable shell was becoming quite heavy and tight.
>
> After a while, in fact, the shell became so cumbersome that the lobster

couldn't feel anything at all outside himself. As a result, he was constantly bumping into others.

Finally, it got to the point where he could hardly even breathe. So with great effort, he went back to see the Creator.

"With all due respect," the lobster sighed, "contrary to what you promised, my shell has not remained the same. It keeps shrinking!"

"Not at all," smiled the Creator. "Your shell may have gotten a little thicker with age, but it has remained the same size. What's happened is that you have changed—inside, beneath your shell."

The Creator continued: "You see, everything changes . . . continuously. No one remains the same. That's the way I've designed things. And the wisest choice is to shed your old shell as you grow."

"I see," said the lobster, "but you must admit it is occasionally inconvenient and a bit uncomfortable."

"Yes," said the Creator, "but remember, all growth carries with it both the possibility of discomfort . . . and the potential for great joy as you discover new parts of yourself. After all, you can't have one without the other."

"That's very sensible," said the lobster.

"If you'd like," offered the Creator, "I'll tell you something more."

"Please do," encouraged the lobster.

"When you let go of your shell and choose to grow," said the Creator, "You build new strength within yourself and in that strength, you'll find new capacity to love yourself . . . to love those around you . . . and to love life itself. That is my plan for each of you."[12]

A climate of growth encourages flexibility—the willingness to try new things. "The willingness to experiment, to innovate, and even to fail are part of flexibility. You cannot program this spirit, nor can you command it, but a few people placed in key positions can model it."[13]

One man modeled this willingness to try new things. The man was dying, and has since died, but he did not want his church of twelve members to die. He worked along with his pastor to have a New Life Mission, an outreach effort coordinated by the General Board of Discipleship, in the church he loved. That effort helped revive the church so that now there are 70 persons in attendance and 15 children in the Sunday school. The man's dream became reality.

A congregation must orient itself toward the future if it expects to grow spiritually. Many people talk about the "good old days." Somehow, we must help people understand that the only "good old days" any of us have are those from here on out into the future!

5. **The congregation's sense of identity.** Some congregations think of themselves as the "prestige church" in town. Some small membership churches think of themselves as a "family church" or perhaps an "extended family." Some churches take their identity from the language spoken or the ethnic makeup of the congregation.

Each church of whatever size, or ethnic, or economic constituency must answer the question in relation to its community, "Are we here to serve or be served?" Each congregation must assess whether or not it has a clearly defined mission statement and concrete missional objectives that put it in creative ministry to its community.

Near a metropolitan area, there exists a white frame church that has stood on the same site for over 175 years. What was a rural church is now surrounded by new housing developments and numerous corporate headquarters housed in multi-storied, lavish brick and stone buildings. The church is immaculately maintained inside and out. A pleasant carpeted nursery area is positioned inside, but no one serves as a regular nursery attendant. A Sunday school is listed on the church sign on the front lawn, but essentially no Sunday school exists except for a few elderly persons. Persons come and go to the primary activity of the white frame church—the Sunday morning worship experience—as they have for decades. The church is located in the midst of a burgeoning population, but will remain oblivious to most of the new residents unless corrective measures are taken and intentional outreach is planned. The church described above is no different from hundreds of churches across America. Many churches in such situations are choosing to remain locked in tradition rather than adopt a changing sense of mission which is demanded by a changing geographical neighborhood.

6. **The congregation's commitment to faith development.** The congregation exists for the faith development of persons—the making of disciples.

The subjective experience of the membership creates and communicates climate in a congregation. When persons worship in joy, warmth, love, and the confidence that they belong to God, the indescribable feeling in that congregation emits a contagious magnetism. This irreducible 'event' com-

municates more to the visitor in the pew than any initiative the church can
take.[14]

A conference staff person in an annual conference in the
South said that he made a visit to one of the churches in the
conference on Sunday morning. His assessment of that service was
conveyed poignantly: "All during that worship experience I kept
looking for the casket." When a feeling of celebration is absent
week after week, stagnation sets in and new persons in a community visit only once before going elsewhere to find their church
home.

In *The Scent of Love,* Keith Miller tells about a surgeon who
supervised younger doctors and interns. A seriously ill man was
admitted to the hospital and a certain intern, anxious to get ahead
and accept tough cases, asked to be assigned to the patient. The
intern was able to get the "temperature down, his fluids in balance,
and his blood count up." Unfortunately, after such a valiant effort,
the patient died. The intern, in anguish, remained in the patient's
room to scribble something on the patient's chart. The supervising
surgeon, looking at the chart, found these words: "This patient was
in better condition when he died than when he first came to me."
As Miller puts it, "I think it's time we quit congratulating each
other on what a good evangelistic program we've had, and ask the
question, 'Are any of the patients still living?'"[15]

The story raises the issue of faith development. Are persons
not only making first-time commitments to Christ in our
churches but also learning how to walk each day with God? When
people get excited about their own journeys of faith in significant
numbers, a contagious climate is present.

7. **The physical structure.** The physical structure, the building, affects the climate for receiving and welcoming new persons
because the state of the building reflects the attitude of the congregation. When the church sign in front has peeling paint and
missing letters, or is overgrown with shrubs, this appearance
communicates something to newcomers driving by the church.
When the nursery is a jumbled mess or located in back of the
boiler room, it communicates something about a congregation's
openness to persons with young children.

Church consultant Lyle Schaller has raised the question numerous times: "What do the written and unwritten 'signs' say?" The outdoor church sign of a large church that has a different shade of paint for each name, relecting frequent staff changes, can communicate a lack of stability that hinders growth. A church sign where the pastor's name hangs from a chain attached to the "main sign" and blows in the wind also suggests something about pastoral continuity and consequently says something about the congregation to observant visitors.

A church consultant was meeting with a congregational planning group in Virginia and raised the question about lack of directions or signs within the church building that would point visitors to the nursery, sanctuary, classrooms, restrooms, or other areas of the church. Apparently the church expected only those persons to attend who had previously been a part of the church and knew where every "nook and cranny" led. The next morning as the consultant arrived to preach the morning service, he found that the associate pastor and his wife had stayed up late or arose early in order to post handmade signs around the church directing persons to classrooms, restrooms, etc.

One large church has thirteen bulletin boards within the church. A volunteer oversees all bulletin boards, but assigns each bulletin board in the church to a different person each month. The bulletin boards have current information, are attractively decorated, and thus "speak" positive messages to numerous visitors who pass up and down the corridors of the church.

In Tullahoma, Tennessee, pastor Edd Templeton intentionally made significant strides in enabling First Church to present a climate of hospitality to visitors. The church office/reception area is purposefully decorated in attractive soft colors with flowers and a coffeepot always available for guests to the office. The pastor's study reflects the same "homey" atmosphere—nice prints, soft colors, and a total mood of relaxation, including a rocking chair. (The pastor explained that persons sometimes come in anxious, especially for a counseling session. When they sit in the rocker and the pace of the rocking slows, he knows they have become more relaxed and are receptive to counseling suggestions!) The entire church, room by room, area by area, has been redone. No longer is there deteriorating paint, inadequate lighting, rusting metal windows, classrooms with leftover curriculum or "mess" in each corner. Now there are attractively painted (carefully chosen colors) and lighted rooms that are more conducive to learning and *hospitality*. The exterior of the church has had the same careful attention to details and renovation, including the stained glass windows and church sign. The shrubs surrounding the church and the lawn remain trimmed. The entire physical facility suggests that the church is alive and that newcomers are expected and welcome!

8. **The congregation's reliance upon God.** Undergirding the previous seven factors is the knowledge that a congregation's reliance upon God affects the climate. When a local congregation understands that it is an outpost of the kingdom of God and continually draws spiritual stamina from a dependence upon God, then faithfulness to the task of making disciples remains firm. Such a congregation understands the promise, "For where two or three are gathered in my name, there am I in the midst of them" (Matthew 18:20, RSV). The congregation understands that the sum is equal to more than the parts, i.e., what the congregation is able to accomplish with God's help is equal to more than the individual gifts of the membership. Such a congregation is always asking, "What is the greatest dream God has for us?"

IV. Assessing the Present Situation in Your Congregation

In Part Two of this book, intentional outreach will be discussed. As a congregation plans for outreach, it must assess its capacity to receive people. The congregation must assess its welcoming posture. In assessing the climate of your church, you can ask present members these questions to be answered by yes or no. (Some questions will not apply to all churches.)

A. Questions related to the attitudes of the membership.	Yes	No
1. Would you like for our church to grow numerically?		
2. Would you be willing for our church to add additional worship services and start new adult classes to accommodate more persons?		
3. Would you be willing personally to invite new residents or friends to unite with our church?		
4. Would you be willing for Sunday school classes to be reassigned to different classroom spaces annually or semiannually to allow some new classes to grow?		
5. Would you support the pastor in his/her desire to spend more time in outreach to new persons and less time calling on existing/long-term members of the church?		
6. Would you be willing for each member to serve on fewer committees or places of leadership in order that new members might have a "voice" and a task in the life of our congregation?		
7. Would you support an increased operating budget allocation for outreach efforts and publicity?		
8. Would you be willing to have a greater variety of music in the worship service to meet the needs of various persons, particularly teenagers and young adults?		
9. Would you be willing to hire a music director/minister to expand the music ministry and allow for more choir or instrumental groupings?		
10. Would you be willing for our church to be placed on a charge with another church or have an extended ministry added to our "station appointment" in order to have a full-time pastor?		

B. Questions related to the welcoming and follow-up of visitors. These questions could be addressed to an evangelism work area, Council on Ministries or Administrative Council, and pastor/staff.	Yes	No
1. Does our church presently have greeters in addition to persons serving as ushers?.............................		
2. Are there persons assigned each Sunday morning to assist persons with handicapping conditions in parking their car or assisting them in and out of a car?....................		
3. Is there a "ritual of friendship" time during the worship service in which members are encouraged to greet guests, as well as each other?		
4. Are visitors contacted by the pastor or staff during the week following their initial visit?...........................		
5. Do lay persons follow up all first-time visitors, preferably within 48 hours of their presence in a Sunday morning worship service?.....................................		
6. Is there a coffee time or other fellowship opportunity following the Sunday worship service for visitors to have a chance to meet members and pastor/staff?		
7. Is there an evangelism contact person in each adult Sunday school class who contacts each visitor to his/her Sunday school class the week following their visit?.............		
8. Is there a brochure or other informative material about the church that can be given to visitors to the church?		
9. Are there scheduled opportunities for visitors to attend inquirers sessions to have their questions about the denomination, Christian commitment, and the church answered?		
10. Are visitors encouraged to sign an attendance pad or guest register on Sundays to secure an adequate name, address, and phone number for follow-up?		
C. The following questions could be asked about the physical setting for ministry. These questions should be answered by the evangelism work area or task group and by other planning groups within the church.	Yes	No
1. Are there parking spaces close to the church for persons with handicapping conditions and also for visitors?...........		
2. Are there signs posted giving clear directions to the sanctuary, restrooms, nursery, classrooms, and fellowship hall? ..		
3. Is the church office or reception area conducive to receiving newcomers to the community inquiring about the church?		

	Yes	No
4. Is there a sign in front of the church that is in good repair with current and correct information on it?............		
5. Is there an adequate nursery?		
6. Is our foyer or fellowship area large enough to allow for informal discussion and/or a coffee time following the morning worship experience?		
7. Do we have adequate space in our sanctuary to encourage the presence of new persons?........................		
8. Is there adequate classroom space to allow for the development of new Sunday school classes or small groups?		
9. Are the hallways and bulletin boards kept attractive and current?		
10. Does the exterior and interior of the church, taken as a whole, invite a return visit from newcomers?...........		
D. The following questions relating to the welcoming and follow-up of visitors could be asked of new members who have joined the church within the last six months to one year.	**Yes**	**No**
1. Were you greeted by persons sitting on the pew with you or around you on your first visit to our church on Sunday?..		
2. Did you receive a personal contact or correspondence from our pastor in the week following your first visit to our church?..		
3. Did you receive a visit or call from lay persons within the church in the week following your first visit to the church?		
4. Did the ushers or greeters make you feel welcome the first time you attended our church?		
5. Was there adequate nearby parking for you when you attended our worship service?.........................		
6. Were there adequate opportunities for you to get acquainted with members before or following the worship service? ...		
7. Were you able to easily find the sanctuary, nursery, classroom, or other area of the church on your first visit to the church?...		
8. If you did not receive follow-up calls or visits during the week following your first visit or did not feel especially welcome your first Sunday, what made you want to return to our church?...		
9. Now that you have been in our church for six months or more, what suggestions do you have to help our church be more welcoming of visitors?........................		

E. Questions related to the image or purpose of the church should also be considered. These questions could be answered by as many persons as possible within the membership of the church.	Yes	No
1. What do you see as the primary purpose of a Christian church?..		
2. What image do you feel our church projects to the community?		
3. When you hear nonmembers of our church talking about our congregation, what do you hear them saying?........		
4. How do you think our total giving in money should be allocated in terms of programming, maintenance, and outreach or missions?		
5. Do you personally feel our church is affecting our community or city as it could or should? Comment on your answer.		
6. Which persons should a church serve?.................		
7. Do you feel our church has a mission/purpose statement?.		
8. If so, how can we help newcomers understand it?........		
9. What could our church do to improve its "grapevine image" in the community?		

V. How Can a Congregation Change the Climate for Outreach?

1. **Assess the situation through congregational self-examination.** Many of the questions raised earlier, and others that a task force or planning group within the church might develop, could be used to get a sense of what church members are thinking and feeling. As questions are not only answered but discussed in various planning groups or open congregational meetings, attitudes surface that are indicators of the present congregational climate.

2. **Identify changes that need to be made.** It may become obvious from various discussions that congregational self-esteem is at a low ebb. Obviously, newcomers looking for a message of hope and spiritual inspiration for the next week are not drawn into a congregation where negativism and despair reign. "In any social grouping, the only quality more contagious than enthusiasm is apathy, and more contagious than apathy is negativism."[16] If self-esteem is low and negativism is prevalent, then what can be done? How can the congregation plan for and achieve one small success which can be celebrated?

Some changes may well include improvements to the physical facility. Perhaps interior direction signs should be posted, the nursery might be "spruced up"; the exterior of the church could be painted; a marquee sign could be placed in front of the church, etc. Again, identifying needed changes is a step toward improving the climate and taking concrete measures to address this area of concern.

3. **Emphasize that spiritual health/formation is necessary for change to take place.** Leaders within a congregation need to include a spiritual dimension in even routine meetings of a church.

While serving on the staff of a church in Colorado Springs, I recall the positive "vibes" that were created when, at the Administrative Board meeting, the question was asked, "Where have you seen God at work since last we met?" Some moving experiences were shared in those moments that helped enliven a meeting with many perfunctory reports and financial statements.

One pastor in New England approached his official body with such a question one month and was met by strong silence. Unperturbed, he raised the same question, "Where have you seen God at work?" at the next month's meeting. Again, strong silence. Though discouraged at the response, he raised the question a third time a month later. One woman responded, "Pastor, you keep asking that question. I don't know exactly what you have in mind, but let me share something that happened in my life." The pastor credits this woman with opening the floodgates of praise and fellowship which, eventually, not only brought new enthusiam and increased attendance at the Board meetings, but spilled over and helped create a more positive climate in the worship services and throughout the congregation.

A medium-sized church has brought a special sense of spirituality into regular choir rehearsals by having choir members relate biblical passages to the hymns that will be sung on Sunday morning. Each choir rehearsal becomes a Bible study as well as a prayer time for one another. When Sunday comes, the hymns that are sung have added meaning for the choir and contribute to the sense of celebration in the service.

4. Use the pulpit to address a needed change. Oftentimes, the pastor plays a significant role in change, especially when there needs to be a change in the image the congregation projects to the community. In one Tennessee church, the pastor aroused curiosity one Sunday by announcing to the congregation: "Next week I will preach one of the most important messages I will ever preach at this church. I want you to be present." The next Sunday the pastor preached on "The Faded Purple." In the sermon, the pastor said this:

> Our church will not live, my friends, because of our location. Our church will not live, my friends, because of our building. Our church will not live because of our senior minister and our staff. Our church will not live because we are still the "in" church. Our church will live because we believe that God has a mission for this church. Without that belief we will have no

soul, no passion for life, no reason for existing. Without that belief that God has a mission for this church, the way will be too narrow, the mountain will be too high, and the winds that oppose us will be too strong. . . .

Our question as a church must simply be this. Do we provide hope for people who come in and out of the doors of this place? The question is no longer, How many people attended the Couples Class this Sunday morning? The question now is, Did the people who attended the Couples Class find hope because they went there? The question is no longer, How many people came to worship? The question is, Did somebody in that worship service this morning find hope because they came? The question is not, How many people used this building from seven in the morning until nine at night? The question is, Do those people find hope because they come here? . . .

Experiencing and offering hope will not make our church into the South's royal church as in days gone by. But it will put us in step with an-other kingdom whose royalty is Christ.

The time has now come in the history of this church for us to exchange the faded purple for a new symbol. The new symbol will not be the purple. The new symbol will need to be more like the butterfly, the opening rose, and the empty tomb, symbolic of new life and new hope."[17]

The pastor or lay person can give sermons or messages, perhaps a series, on the purpose of the church. There is no excuse for any church not trying to relate positively to its community in the present tense.

5. **Approach needed changes in a positive way.** Any church should approach its internal congregational life in as positive a way as possible. Planning should include steps to identify the strengths of a church, and how those strengths can be expanded and en-hanced. Where gaps exist—where changes should be made to enhance the congregational climate—those changes should be interpreted positively. The pastor or other leader needs to say: "These are changes that need to happen in order for our congrega-tion to more effectively minister to this community and strengthen some of the good things we are already doing."

When corrective measures are needed after intentional con-gregational analysis, establish the committee or task force respon-sible for implementing the necessary changes and establish a timeline to see that certain things are accomplished within a reasonable time frame. Like other planning that takes place within a church, the "what," "why," "when," "where," "how," and "who" questions need to be answered so that responsibility and account-ability for action can be understood by all concerned. Changes that will improve the climate for outreach must be interpreted as necessary to allow the church to be a more vital center of Christian mission.

6. **Concentrate on improving all that happens in the Sunday morning worship experience.** All that happens from the time visitors park to enter the church building until they leave the premises after the worship service is supremely important. What happens in the worship "hour" as people sit listening to the choir, hearing the sermon, and participate in various aspects of the liturgy cannot be overestimated. William H. Willimon and Robert L. Wilson, in *Preaching and Worship in the Small Church,* state:

> Small churches will recover their own unique sense of mission and will restore their positive self-image only when they recover and boldly claim the fundamental significance of Sunday for their congregational life and for the life of the universal church. Small churches may not be equipped to do some of the jobs larger churches have taken upon themselves in recent years, but they are fully prepared to proclaim and to celebrate the Word, to care for and edify the body of Christ, and to foster, in Richard Niebuhr's memorable phrase, an "increase of the love of God and neighbor." The fulfillment of the theological purpose of the church never requires a crowd.[18]

What happens in the worship service, as has already been stressed, depends not only on what is happening in the altar and pulpit area or choir loft, but what is happening in the minds and hearts of persons in the congregation as they gather for worship on Sunday. What is the climate in which the worship service takes place?

> The sense of warmth and winsomeness is the first thing to be discerned as one studies the ways in which members and constituents relate to one another before, during, and after the service of worship. Do members of the congregation have a sense of grace? Do they operate from a theology of love? Do the people in the church evidence that they are the body of Christ in community one with another? Do the people who are members and constituents share a fellowship as Christian friends—a fellowship that shares with them strength and help and hope?[19]

7. **Use the nominating committee to help bring about change.** Sometimes the changes that are needed in a congregation's life can only be realized if there is a change in leadership (sometimes a change in pastoral leadership, but many times a change in a few lay leadership positions). In small membership

churches, where persons have held leadership positions for a long time, sometimes out of necessity, those changes do not happen without discomfort and some difficulty. No pastor or sensitive lay person intentionally wants to hurt another person, and make that other person feel undesirable or unloved. Yet, because the church must face the future, the changes must occur. Thus leadership changes may call for corresponding lay and pastoral care to a person who may feel hurt by needed changes. Forward-looking visionary leadership is too vital for congregational climate to routinely fill church offices with merely anyone.

> The beauty is that a growth climate does not have to wait for action by the official board. One individual can begin to model the components of this climate and have an incredible influence. Obviously, when church leaders are the models, growth can happen more quickly. But any person can be the first line of influence.
>
> I recall sitting in a restaurant on Christmas Day. I went in expecting the atmosphere to be grim. After all, who wants to work on Christmas? Much to my surprise, it was almost like walking in on a party. One waitress had obviously decided that if she was going to have to work, she would make the best of it. She had bells tied on her shoes and was joking with customers. She was having a great time, and thanks to her, so was everyone else in the restaurant!
>
> Perhaps that is what it takes in each of our churches—one or two people determined to influence the climate of the church. We may not be able to change weather conditions, but when it comes to the church atmosphere, we can not only survive the elements but adjust them to help the harvest.[20]

The order in which persons are nominated can affect the lay leadership of a congregation. Personal experience suggests that often local church nominating committees nominate lay leaders, trustees, the finance committee, the lay delegate to annual meetings, and the treasurer early in the nominating process. Near the end of the nominating procedure, "slots" that still need to be filled include evangelism, worship, and stewardship chairpersons (some of those less important offices in certain persons' minds). Of course, the lay leaders, treasurers, and trustees are important, but what about the leadership necessary to direct the important work areas of the church or the chairpersons of outreach and membership care in the Administrative Council structure. What if the evangelism, Christian education, stewardship, and worship chairpersons were nominated *first!* Better still, what if a local congregation placed an emphasis upon every person discovering his/her gifts for ministry, in order that each person could serve the church effectively by using his/her own unique gifts?[21] Perhaps persons serving on the finance committee could best serve on an evangelism task force or vice versa. We sometimes assume that people have only one spiritual gift or one interest. If a person is a banker, then automatically he/she is placed on the finance committee, or if a person is a teacher, he/she is usually approached to be on the Christian education work area. While there is certainly some logic for assuming such correlations between vocation in life and leadership positions in the church, it may well be that a teacher who relates to students every day, for example, is just the kind of relational person needed to coordinate a visitation program within a church. When persons serve the church in a capacity that they enjoy, as well as one for which they are equipped, they make a positive contribution to congregational life. And when leaders model a growth climate, it is contagious!

8. **Celebrate positive changes.** In some churches the celebration of a victory is absent.

> It is my conviction that the crisis of the local church is primarily an attitudinal one. Negative expectations tend to produce self-fulfilling prophecies of despair. What is missed . . . is the excitement and joy of projections about possibilities, potentialities, opportunities, and resources. Needed is the celebration of some victories, even small ones, which God will give when persons are receptive in faith.[22]

If a church is intentional about changing attitudes, some victories will come. Then celebration is the appropriate response. If the exterior or interior of the church has been renovated to present some signs of "aliveness," then publicly recognize the persons responsible and as a congregation celebrate the "newness." If the education work area in a small membership church has enabled a second adult class to be organized, where previously there was only one class, then celebrate the fact that now there is a port of entry for additional persons into the life of the congregation. If the men's group has replaced the decaying sign in front of the church with a well-lit brick and wrought iron sign proudly displaying the name of the church, then celebrate that achievement.

Celebrate even small victories or accomplishments. Cultivate the attitude of gratitude!

9. **Conduct an annual audit of the congregation's climate.** By assessing your congregation's climate one time and then assuming all is well or will be, you may make a mistake. The assessment needs to be made periodically to see that the congregation is progressing in displaying a welcoming posture for newcomers and is open to including those persons in the fellowship of the congregation. Ezra Earl Jones and James D. Anderson suggest an annual face-to-face audit of a congregation's human and emotional climate. They suggest auditing these areas of inquiry:

1) Is reflection on one's individual religious pilgrimage a valued congregational activity? . . .
2) Is corporate reflection on the impact, the actual transforming influence of the congregational life, honored, valued, and performed?
3) What stories do we tell about ourselves?
4) To what degree can the congregation tolerate differences?
5) Does membership in the church simply bring more busyness and activity, or does it instead provide space in the normal rounds of life?
6) Is it acceptable to express affection or anger in the course of a church meeting? . . .
One of the most practical and attainable leadership objectives is to make it acceptable to engage in a searching, fruitful evaluation of church life and practice.[23]

10. **Look to the future.** Each congregation needs to see its potential rather than rehearse its problems! The beginning point in looking toward the future might be the adoption of several projects which will cause the congregation to interact positively with people in its community.

Mission leads us beyond ourselves. Whenever a local congregation is effectively engaged in missional outreach, that congregation is a group of people living beyond their preoccupation with themselves. Precisely because they live beyond themselves, their strengths are commensurately developed, their vision is substantially lifted, and their energies are vitalized to new levels of living.[24]

There is no way to separate what happens outside the sanctuary walls from the spirit, the climate, that pervades the life of the gathered congregation.

Ingrown never equals growing. Many churches establish an anti-growth climate without even realizing it by allowing their predominant focus to become the needs of those already in the church. . . . The minute we start to plan for others rather than for ourselves we create a climate where we develop and the church will grow.

Every step we take to facilitate ministry to those outside our congregation causes us to struggle past our own comfort.[25]

As a congregation plans for ministry to and with hurting humanity, the momentum of ministry carries the congregation into the future!

Part Two:
Extending the Welcoming Fellowship

I. What Type of Church Are We?

Not long ago a St. Louis church sent out the weekly bulletin which contained this announcement, "Our church to be sold." Fortunately, the church was not going out of existence, for the following paragraphs elaborated on the heading:

> YES! Our church is to be sold! No, we are not about to lose our building through foreclosure or repudiated debt. However, our church must be sold to the city and the county. It has been planted to wield an influence beyond its membership and walls. Thus, we are presented with an enormous challenge. Our church must be sold to the unchurched! There are scores of people in our community who would attend our church and join us in the Lord's service if we would bother to sell our church to them.[1]

Many congregations need to take more seriously the idea of presenting the message of Christ to the unchurched! Your church is probably one of two types of churches—either the "Little Bo Peep church" or the "Good Shepherd church." The Little Bo Peep church knows the nursery rhyme:

> Little Bo Peep has lost her sheep
> and doesn't know where to find them.
> But leave them alone
> and they'll come home
> wagging their tails behind them.[2]

The Little Bo Peep church has a sign on the front lawn with the times of services posted and the pastor's study in the church is designated. If a person wants to know Christ and know about the Christian way of life, let him/her show up at the appropriate time for worship or call to make an appointment to see the pastor. In other words, we wait for people to come to us.

But the "Good Shepherd church," on the other hand, understands the story of the good shepherd in the Bible and realizes that the church—the people who make up the congregation—are

30

called to follow the lead of Christ and reach out to persons even before they turn their footsteps toward the church. In the Bible, the good shepherd leaves the sheep at some risk in the wilderness in order to seek the one sheep that is lost. The Christian congregation is always called to become vulnerable for the sake of persons who are not in a positive dynamic relationship with God. The church is always called upon to lose itself for the sake of the world. "For whoever would save his life will lose it, and whoever loses his life for my sake will find it" (Matthew 16:25, RSV).

It is easy to become content with the status quo in our churches. It's great to see the same familiar faces week after week, and if we are not careful, we draw our fellowship circle smaller and smaller. Unconsciously, if not intentionally, we exclude new persons. A woman in a Presbyterian congregation said recently:

> We are sometimes guilty of not speaking to visitors after the service because we are so busy talking to those we know. Moreover, isn't it easier to speak to the nice-looking couple sitting near you rather than to the elderly man or woman sitting a row or two from you? One thing that gets to me is hearing someone say, "I don't know if that person is new or one who's been here longer than I have." It doesn't matter; one should speak to them.

At other times we talk about "renewal" in our churches, but too often such talk reflects a surface desire to become more spiritual without making any significant change in our individual life or our corporate way of doing things. Renewal, thus, becomes an impossibility.

"The trap which must be avoided is 'getting stuck' in renewal and never reaching out to new persons. Renewal can become a nondirectional, dead-end street. Consequently, while you develop strategies for the renewal of the church, begin also to develop plans for outreach."[3]

In other words, a congregation cannot wait until everything is "perfect" in its interior corporate life before attempting to reach out.

At this point we are primarily talking about outreach which results in Christian discipleship and church membership. However, all outreach to persons does *not* have to end in their joining our church. In fact, ministry needs to happen for the sake of other persons, regardless of their response. A church that attempts only those things that will build up the budget or membership statistics has missed its calling to be a servant to its community.

Your congregation must inevitably discover that many people are attracted to a church that meets their physical, spiritual, and emotional needs and/or the needs of members of their family. Ministry is always for the sake of persons and not for the sake of the institution. Intentional sustained outreach is planned; ports of entry into the life of a congregation are created; and incorporation is structured in order that individuals might have more abundant, meaningful lives. Growth is not sought so that the monthly receipts will balance expenditures or the monthly membership report sent to the district office will look impressive. Growth is a by-product of compassion and concern for persons in community.

II. Biblical Imperative for Reaching Out

Nearly every book related to evangelism refers to Jesus' Great Commission as the basis for reaching out.

> And Jesus came and said to them, "All authority in heaven and on earth has been given to me. Go therefore and make disciples of all nations, baptizing them in the name of the Father and of the Son and of the Holy Spirit, teaching them to observe all that I have commanded you; and lo, I am with you always, to the close of the age."
>
> (Matthew 28:18-20, RSV)

Indeed, no one can ignore that command. But there are other verses and stories in the Bible that give guidance to us in searching for biblical undergirding for our work. Most persons have heard many times about the parable of the prodigal son in Luke 15. But that parable took on new meaning following our son's graduation from college. He was awarded a self-directed study in languages which called for him to spend six months to a year in Europe, particularly among people who spoke Catalan. While our son was not "squandering his life," he was literally in a far country. He had never been to Europe, nor had we, his parents. The day came when he took the flight to New York and on to Frankfurt, Germany. There was no travel agent to help arrange an itinerary, so we were left with a tentative schedule saying roughly on what dates he might be reached through the American Express office in Barcelona, Spain or Lisbon, Portugal or Florence, Italy. With some books and all the clothes that would fit in one large knapsack that could be carried from one youth hostel to another, from one city to another throughout Europe, he began his journey alone.

His mother and I worried a lot about his whereabouts and his safety, and if a long-distance call, a letter, or postcard from some country did not arrive about every ten days, we became very anxious. In fact, on one occasion when we had not heard from our son for a while, I was mentally setting out my own itinerary in

Europe where I might fly and begin to find him. It was then that the parable of the prodigal son grasped me. I understand the action of the father in the parable, especially as that biblical father figure kept his eyes toward the road for the return of his son. ("But while he was yet at a distance, his father saw him and had compassion, and ran and embraced him and kissed him"; Luke 15:20, RSV).

Those of us who are fortunate enough to have more than one child, might theoretically be asked the question, "Which child do you love the most?" Thinking that to be a totally insensitive question, we would answer: "Why, what do you mean, we love all of our children the same." That would be the correct answer. But in a real sense, I believe we could also answer with some truthfulness, "We love the most the child who is farthest away from home at any given time or the one who is ill at the moment." I will never forget the agonizing moments my wife and I spent when we, incorrectly it turned out, were led to believe our young daughter might have an incurable illness. Any parent who has sat by the bedside of a seriously ill child knows the love extended and expressed in those days of watching and waiting. In such a situation a parent not only *looks at his or her child but watches* the child for any glimmer of improvement and hope.

Like a parent, God loves all God's children the same. But I cannot help but believe that the heavenly Parent has a special longing, a special concern for every child who is spiritually and perhaps morally in a "far country." We are told that there is great joy in heaven over one returning child: even as there was feasting at the return of the younger child in the parable (Luke 15:7).

The biblical mandate is to share the Good News of God's love with all persons, not just our own relatives or people "like us." Ultimately, we are able to extend love because we have experienced it. "In this is love, not that we loved God but that he loved us and sent his Son to be the expiation for our sins. Beloved, if God so loved us, we also ought to love one another" (1 John 4:10-11, RSV).

III. The Purpose of the Church

An effective Christian congregation of any size can be defined with five tasks: Reach, Receive, Relate, Develop, and Send.[4] An effective congregation is one that reaches out to persons as they are, not as we wish they were; receives those persons into the membership and fellowship circles of the congregation; with the presence and power of the Holy Spirit relates those persons to God; develops them as disciples; and then sends them back out into the larger community to make it more loving and just, a better place in which to live. The cycle of reaching unchurched, undiscipled persons and sending out transformed individuals is also what it means to "make disciples." *Making* disciples does not imply that the effort is all ours but that in actuality *God* makes disciples through God's church and the individual members that comprise it.

The business world already approaches its mission in a similar way. A McDonald's hamburger ad states:

McDonald's People. Serving Customers and the Community.
　　To McDonald's, people are everything.
　　Not only the people who work for us, but the people we serve as well.
　　The truth is, commitment, drive, and talent are what make McDonald's people special . . .
　　It's really all a matter of *pride*.
　　So it's not surprising that the people who take pride in their work at McDonald's are also proud to serve the community.[5]

The ad is a reminder that certain businesses pay more attention to their community and customers than churches pay to their community and to those persons who need to understand that they are recipients of grace.

Each congregation might read a scripture passage, such as Acts 3:1-10, and discuss it in light of its community. The story recorded in Acts is about Peter and John going into the temple to pray, when they were asked by a lame man for alms. In this particular story, Peter responded that they had no silver and gold, but they were agents bringing a better gift—healing. "And he [Peter] took him by the right hand and raised him up; and immediately his feet and ankles were made strong. And leaping up he stood and walked and entered the temple with them, walking and leaping and praising God" (Acts 3:7-8, RSV). As a congregation, ask, "Who are the lame persons at our gate, and how can we bring healing to them so that they too might praise God?" The lame persons at your church's gate may not be literally physically lame, but there are barriers, impediments in persons' lives that prevent them from having the more abundant life in Christ.

A church must extend open arms, a welcoming embrace, to those who are "lame" and help raise them up so that they can stand on their own feet, carry their own burdens. Sometimes the church is the builder of the barriers before persons, such as when it stresses stringent requirements before persons can even participate in the fellowship of the congregation. One biblical invitation states: "And let him who is thirsty come, let him who desires take the water of life without price" (Revelation 22:17, RSV). If a church is to make disciples, obviously some demands must be placed on the individual. But if we, as Christians, really believe that persons will have a better chance of meeting Christ within the church than outside it, and more opportunities to grow in discipleship in the church rather than outside it, then the entrance should be fairly wide open into the life and fellowship of a congregation so that many opportunities can be given within the church to strengthen one's faith journey. David Lowes Watson pictures the church as "a porous membrane where muscle is provided inside." In other words, entrance into the fellowship can begin at once, but Bible study, covenant discipleship groups, Sunday school classes, etc., provide the "muscle" for new Christians. The concept could be diagrammed as on the following page.

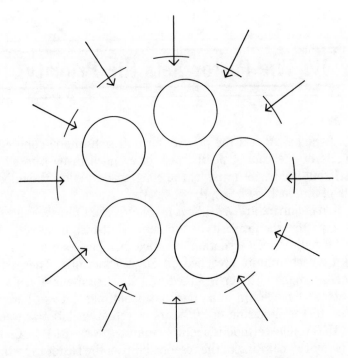

If such a concept of the church stirs our imagination, then we are called to extend intentionally the welcoming fellowship and practice the posture of hospitality to newcomers.

IV. The Pastor Sets the Priority

The pastor sets the priority for outreach in any congregation. He or she cannot do the task of evangelism by himself or herself, but the pastor must let the congregation know the importance of outreach by being the pacesetter.

Ken Callahan, in *Twelve Keys to an Effective Church,* suggests that a pastor should visit newcomers, shut-ins, inactives, the hospitalized, or even visitation of active members one hour each week for each minute preached on Sunday morning. The pastor either has many visits or is forced into short sermons! Even as a Minister of Evangelism in a previous appointment, it was hard to live up to the guideline of 20 hours of actual visitation a week, since the average sermon is about 20 minutes. Nevertheless, Callahan is right in pointing to the responsibility of the pastor in setting priorities within the congregation.[6]

H. Eddie Fox tells about a visit from the lay leader in a church he served. He was only in his new appointment for a few weeks when the lay leader came into the pastor's study and said, "Eddie, if you don't know more about running this church than I know about being a lay leader, we are in serious trouble."

Eddie replied, "If you take your *Discipline* down from the shelf and turn to the job description of the lay leader, you will see that the lay leader is responsible for recruiting five or six other lay persons and meeting with the pastor in his or her study each Monday night before visiting in homes."

The lay leader responded, "The nominating committee didn't explain the job to me that way."

Eddie grinned and clarified, "The *Discipline* doesn't really say that, but that is what I would like for you to do!"

The lay leader responded positively (fortunately for Eddie). Each Monday visits were made to newcomers and other persons. To inform the congregation of the priority of visitation, a message was announced to the people that no one should schedule a meeting on Monday night if he/she expected the pastor or lay leader to be present. They would not be available because of prior commitments.

V. Each Congregation Needs to Answer These Questions

Answer these questions in your congregation if you are intentional about reaching out to other persons. Such questions include the following:

1. What is the "glue" that is holding our congregation together?

The glue, says Lyle Schaller, is the "basic organizing principle that holds a congregation together." He states: "Every long-established congregation is organized around one or more principles which weld a loose collection of individuals into a cohesive group . . . some members may be tied to that particular congregation by two or three components of the glue which keep potential members from joining."[7] The glue may be denominational identity, ethnic language and culture, kinfolk ties, social class, theological stance, nostalgia, the liturgy, the pastor, or a number of other factors. When a congregation understands the glue that is holding it together, then persons can determine who might logically be attracted to that congregation or what factors need to be addressed if changes are to occur and the congregation become more "welcoming."

2. What do we have to declare?

The emphasis here is not on evangelizing the Good News, which *each church* should do, but upon the particular strengths of a particular congregation that are worth sharing with others. What is the congregation doing that is noteworthy? It is more helpful to identify strengths and expand those strengths than it is to point continually to areas where the church is weak or has little possibility of ministry. A congregation must deal with problems, but somehow they must also emphasize what's *right* with the church. A Sunday school class for retarded persons, the sponsoring of a refugee family, the establishment of a counseling center in the church facility, and countless other things may be something to celebrate in a community. Sometimes persons are attracted to a church not because of a particular emphasis or program, but because the church is *demonstrating a caring attitude.* That climate of concern attracts persons like a magnet.

Each church periodically needs to assess its strengths. Maybe the question could be asked this way: "If our church suddenly were to be closed, who in the community would miss it, and why?"

3. Who are we intentionally trying to reach?

Start with the demographic data that indicate who lives in a local church's community. Age, family makeup, and other factors may give direction to a congregation which is seeking to relate positively to its community. No single church can reach everyone in any community. Studies indicate that young adults born after World War II tend to affiliate more with large churches, perhaps because of an expansive program or the possibility that such churches will include in their membership large numbers of young adults who are children of long-time members. At any rate, every church cannot hope to meet the needs of a great number of single young adults. A congregation should make every effort to reach out to its entire community, at the same time realizing that the "glue" that holds it together may unintentionally exclude some persons.

4. Who, unconsciously, are we excluding?

Some churches are excluding persons who do not need to be excluded. More and more, churches are making their facilities accessible to persons with handicapping conditions. In some inner-city areas, churches may be excluding persons who speak a different language when a service or even another congregation could be started for those persons in the existing church facility. Alternative worship services have also proven effective in meeting the spiritual needs of persons who respond to different liturgies. A church planning group needs to ask *intentionally,* "Who are we excluding *unintentionally?*"

5. What attracting events or ministries are being planned to

involve persons in our congregation who would not normally appear on Sunday morning?

When I was growing up in a Methodist church in Memphis, those attracting events were a pancake breakfast, ice cream social, spaghetti dinner, or fish fry. Such events enabled members to invite others to a nonthreatening social environment. As guests came, they discovered that the members were fun to be around and it might even be okay to worship with them!

One church in the Midwest for many years held a "Great Tree Service," the first Sunday night of Advent. It was a festive time at which a number of choirs would sing, Christmas carols were sung by the congregation, and everything prepared persons to move outside the sanctuary for the closing portion of the service. Outside, on the church lawn, a great tree had been brought down from the Rocky Mountains (a tree was later *planted* in front of the church for ecological reasons) and decorated with 2,000 lights. At the appropriate time, a senior citizen (chosen each year) would plug in the tree. As those 2,000 lights sprang to illumination, the gathered congregation would shout "Let there be light!" For the rest of the Christmas season that tree became, in a sense, Colorado Springs' Christmas tree. After the lighting of the tree, everyone was invited into the church's fellowship hall for hot cider and other refreshments. The "Great Tree Service" attracted much attention and was a marvelous opportunity for members to invite friends or relatives to the church.

First Church, Colorado Springs, also planned other efforts that served as attracting events for new persons. For many years the church held an outdoor worship service in the summer months at a drive-in theater. The service was called "Cowboy Church" because of the western motif surrounding the service. For example, the offering was received from cars by persons on horseback. Prayer requests were also turned in at that time. Persons drove their vans or cars into the drive-in, turned on the speakers, and participated in an unusual worship service and setting. If persons particularly liked a sermon or song being sung, they could not say "amen" or clap, but they could blow their car horns, and they did! While such a service might seem like a gimmick to some people, needs were still being met. One day a prayer request card was placed in the offering plate which said: "Thank you for having this service. My husband is a paraplegic and is never able to attend church. We can put him in the back of our van and bring him here. He enjoys the service so much."

Always keep in mind that ministering to personal needs should come before recruitment for membership. For example, a church in Alabama established a ministry called "Friends for Life," as part of their nursery ministry.

Friends for Life—will be a specialized ministry to children with handicapping conditions and special needs, and to their families. Some people in our church have discovered that whenever a couple is pregnant and learn they might have a handicapped child, the resources to which that family might turn are very limited in Montgomery. Doctors have indicated an interest in some kind of support group to whom they could refer these families. This new ministry is an outgrowth of that need. We have discovered that parents who have a handicapped child are very reluctant to leave that child in the nursery. Oftentimes volunteer helpers are afraid that they might 'do something wrong' for the child. This ministry is going to train nursery workers who can have a special ministry to these children.

One of the opportunities will be to train babysitters for handicapped children. Parents of children with special needs indicate that it is very difficult to find someone whom they can trust. There are also plans to have a Friday night out for parents through which trained nursery workers will be available here at the church to care for children with special needs, as well as their brothers and sisters. Parents need to have a sense of confidence in the kind of care their children will receive when they leave them.[8]

This ministry will attract new persons to the church, but that is not the reason for inaugurating the ministry. This rapidly growing church looks for unmet needs in the larger Montgomery community and moves to establish ministries to meet whatever needs might surface, provided that the church can supply volunteer help to respond adequately to the need.

Other attracting ministries might include mental health seminars, divorce recovery workshops, cancer therapy groups, parents without partners groups, or even a softball team. Such efforts are offered to meet specific needs in a community, because a holistic approach then enables a congregation to invite persons to participate in the total life of the congregation, including Sunday worship and all aspects of the church.

What attracting events or ministries are being planned to

involve people in your congregation who would not normally appear on Sunday morning?

6. What happens when a person visits our church?

How do we welcome and follow up on guests to our church? Almost every church growth consultant confirms that following up on first-time visitors with a personal visit or contact within 24-48 hours of their visiting a church for the first time enhances greatly the chances of those persons visiting a church again and, in fact, eventually uniting with that church. When lay persons help follow up visitors, there is an even better chance that those visitors will return to a church.

Of course, welcoming guests to a church begins before, during, and after the worship service itself. In one California church, first-time visitors are recognized in the worship service and presented with a potted plant that contains a wooden fish symbol. The two great commandments mentioned by Jesus are carved on each side of the wood ("Love God with all your heart, soul, mind, and strength," and "Love your neighbor as yourself"). Church members obviously know who first-time visitors are and have no excuse for not welcoming a person carrying a potted plant!

Other churches also follow up first-time visitors with a visit that includes a symbolic object. A church in the Midwest has lay persons take a small loaf of bread to visitors. In a doorstep visit they suggest: "Come share the bread of life with us." Other churches carry out to the home a green sprig in a pot with the admonition: "Come grow with us." Across the country, various churches are now taking out freshly baked pies to new residents in the community who visit their church. In Hawaii, a church felt that the appropriate item for new residents to the island might be a fresh pineapple! In East Tennessee, a church contemplated taking apple butter to first-time visitors. Such visible expressions of caring can be extremely meaningful to recipients.

In California, a man in desperation decided to take his own life by jumping off the Golden Gate bridge. He was determined to drive 50 miles to the bridge, then end his life. On the way to the bridge his truck broke down, but he continued to walk toward the bridge.

The longer he walked, the louder an inner voice seemed to say, "God doesn't want you to take your life." The fact that his truck had broken down seemed to confirm that inner voice. He later found a Bible and read John 3:16. He determined that perhaps he ought to go to a church, and he remembered some positive things that he had heard about one nearby.

He attended that church on a Sunday morning. On Monday evening some visitors from the church brought him a freshly baked pie as they customarily do for first-time visitors. The man was so overcome by this display of welcome that he decided to attend a midweek inquirers' class led by the pastor of the church. The next Sunday when the invitation was given, the man came down the aisle and committed his life to Christ.

At another church, persons were seeking to have their church become more intentional in outreach. Forty persons volunteered one Sunday to bake pies to take to visitors. Another nearby church decided to go a similar route and to use Heritage Sunday and the necessity of "spreading the Word" to challenge the membership to become more involved in outreach. On Heritage Sunday, ten freshly baked pies were in the narthex for visitors, but this display also stimulated members to bake pies and offer expressions of caring.

In a small membership church, the greeting of a newcomer in the service is extremely important. In a church with few visitors, members may be "out of the habit" of greeting guests and tend to form small cliques unto themselves before or after the service, to exchange community news. Lay persons *and* the pastor must see that visitors are included in "single-cell" churches. Of course, the follow-up visit during the week is still a crucial aspect of follow-through to newcomers. In small membership churches, the follow-up procedure will not be as elaborate as in other size churches and thus will depend upon the careful and thoughtful approach by the pastor and one or two key lay persons.

In a large membership church, the process of follow-up to visitors will involve a number of persons and various avenues of contact and communication. For example, that process might look like this:

1. Visitors sign the attendance pad in the worship services.
2. Visitors are also encouraged to sign a visitor's card, putting one portion in the offering plate, affixing the other portion to their garment.
3. Church greeters greet visitors before and after services.
4. Attendance pad sheets are torn out and taken to the office work area following the Sunday services, where "Cut-Ups" separate names into members, in-town visitors, out-of-town visitors, wish call, etc.
5. All in-town names are separated into alphabetical order. The Minister of Evangelism or Visitation Coordinator receives a list on Monday morning of all in-town visitors.
6. All in-town visitor names are sent by mail by Monday to Minutewomen/Minutemen, who telephone each person or family. A duplicate record is kept of all contacts. One copy goes to the Visitation Coordinator or the Minister of Evangelism; the other copy is retained for information for the telephone lay caller. In this way, the telephone caller, as well as the Visitation Coordinator/Minister of Evangelism, knows about the repeat visits to the church by a person. Telephone callers are to phone visitors before the following Sunday.
7. Persons checking "new resident" or "wish a call" are visited Sunday afternoon. The goal is for lay persons and/or pastors to visit all first-time visitors or those with special needs before the next Sunday. Lay persons visit in teams or individually. A note from the Minister of Evangelism is sent to persons where only a box number is available.
8. After contacts reveal that persons are interested in church membership or wish to learn more about Christianity and the church, they are urged to attend membership orientation classes.
9. In membership orientation, persons learn more about what it means to be a Christian, the meaning of commitment and church membership, and are given an overview of the denomination's history and beliefs. Persons fill out interest indicators and estimate-of-giving cards as part of the orientation process.
10. Persons desiring to unite with the church are received into

membership at the altar of the church. Each person signs his or her name in the church membership book.

11. New-member receptions are held periodically for new members to become better acquainted with staff and key lay personnel in the church and vice versa.

12. All new members are assigned an area number according to the geographical area in which they live. They become part of a neighborhood plan.

13. All new members, as a group or as individuals, are encouraged to become part of the "Network," a neighborhood group plan for small sharing groups.

14. All new members are invited to a coffee at the home of the senior pastor, usually in groups of approximately 15 persons. Information taken in the home at these new-member coffees is given to each professional staff member and lay chairpersons of work areas or committees.

15. Follow through is done by staff and lay persons to help people find their place in the life of the church. A secretary in charge of assimilation coordinates contacts.

16. Follow-up contacts on new members are made by members of the Stewardship Work Area or by pastors on the staff.

While serving as Minister of Evangelism on a large church staff, I instituted a series of referral cards by which various departments in the church reported and followed up on guests to their activities and I, in turn, referred persons, many of whom had already visited the church, to various Sunday school classes, choirs, and youth groups. A sample of those referral cards follows.

Church School Department Card

CHURCH SCHOOL DEPARTMENT
*(see both sides of card)

To: Rev. Jim Cowell

From: Church School Classes (Department)

Subject: In-town visitors to class.

The following person(s), who live in Colorado Springs, were visiting the _____ name of class class on _____ date .

Name	Address	Phone (if known)	1st visit	2nd visit	3rd visit	Frequent visitor

(over)

Our teacher or church school class members made the following contact outside of class with the person(s) listed, encouraging them to be a part of First United Methodist Church, with the following results:

_____

_____

_____

_____

_____

Signed _____ date

Referral Card

REFERRAL CARD
*(see both sides of card)

To: _____

From: Rev. Jim Cowell

Subject: Referral _____ Date _____

The following person(s) need to be contacted by your department:

Name _____

Address _____

Phone _____

They are a ____ prospective member of the church
____ member of the church

They desire the following information:

_____

After contacting this person (or these persons) report on your contact on the back of this card and return to me.

I, or my department, contacted the named persons on the front of this card on _____ date , with the following result:

_____

_____

_____

_____

_____

_____

signed _____ date

7. Can our congregation help sponsor another new congregation?

Sponsoring another congregation may not necessarily bring more new members into the *existing church,* but revitalizing the interior life of a congregation is directly related to outreach. A church intent on keeping its money and limits of concern within the "four walls" usually finds that the congregation dies spiritually. Spiritually dying churches may even cease to exist as organized communities of faith. An existing church can sponsor another new church by fulfilling several roles—including providing the nucleus of members for a new congregation, making available its facilities to be used by a new congregation, loaning out a staff person to assist in organizational efforts, financially undergirding a new congregation and assisting in other ways. (See *Sponsoring New Congregations* by W. James Cowell, Discipleship Resources.)[9]

Sometimes outreach efforts initiated by a congregation will not result in a new *chartered* congregation but will result in significant ongoing mission groups, such as outpost Sunday schools in housing projects, trailer courts, or high-rise apartment dwellings. (See Kirk McNeill, *Start-Up Manual for New Sunday Schools,* Discipleship Resources.)[10] Because of socioeconomic factors, some persons who need the fellowship of other Christians will *not* come to an existing church but will respond to a new grouping in their own familiar environment.

8. Are we doing any long-range planning related to growth and outreach?

What would your congregation like to see happen in the next year? Five years? Ten years? If numerical growth is expected and being planned, growth may mean a corresponding increase in square footage of building space available, a second or third worship service, increased staff, more varied intentional efforts to incorporate new persons, etc. If special preaching events or short-term faith-sharing training sessions are being planned, these need to be announced well in advance, materials ordered, and preparations made to see that events are not only "announced" but proceed with attendance secured. *If an event or training session is worth scheduling, it should be worth the effort of securing attendance!*

A concrete way to plan for the future is to look at the five tasks which describe an effective congregation: reach, receive, relate, develop, and send. Each congregation can ask of each task, "What are we now doing in this area?" Then the congregation could ask, "What more could we be doing in this area?"

For example, the question could be asked, "What are we now doing to incorporate (receive) persons into the fellowship of our congregation?" After some discussion, the question could then be asked, "What more can we do to help persons feel a part of our congregation?" Future directions will surface from a realistic appraisal of present ministry.

Any church serious about its evangelistic outreach could use *Evangelism Ministries: Planning Handbook* with an existing committee or form a task force to specifically work through that resource and make concrete *plans*.[11] It can never be overemphasized, however, that evangelism/outreach is the responsibility of the whole congregation.

VI. Encouraging the Membership to Invite Others

One of the most important things any person can do is to invite other persons to attend his/her church. The 1988 study of *The Unchurched American* by the Gallup Organization revealed:

> 58% of the unchurched said they would "definitely," "probably," or "possibly" return to church, up from 52% in 1978. . . . Invitation and evangelism are virtually ignored by the "mainline" churches, certainly an important reason many of these churches have lost members in the last decade or two.
>
> The 1988 survey shows that one American in three (34%) has been asked to become active in a church or synagogue other than their own in the past year, with 8 in 10 of this group asked more than once. About half of those approached to join a church say their response to the invitation, or invitations, was favorable?[12]

Note the following report:

> The phone call came on Friday afternoon. It was long distance. A lady's charming voice said, "I want to thank you and the people . . . because through your church the eternal destiny of me and my husband was changed." Wow! That is some way to start a conversation.
>
> She went on to share how she and her husband were eating in a restaurant about a year ago. A gentleman and his family were seated at the table next to them. They politely spoke, and then the man engaged her and her husband in a moment of conversation. He inquired where they went to church, and they admitted that they had not been to church in years. He invited them to church.
>
> The lady said that she and her husband attended, somewhat out of curiosity, but felt something in that service of worship that they had never felt before. They continued to come for a few Sundays, and in the privacy of their home made a commitment to Jesus Christ. They were transferred at that time, and they have become active in a church in a different state.
>
> She kept saying, "That man's simple invitation changed our eternal destiny." Think about that—one little invitation that changed an eternal destiny. Eternity is a long, long time—in fact, it is forever. She kept offering thanks for that invitation of that man. . . .
>
> One simple invitation. What did you talk about the last time you went out to dinner? What do you talk about at the office, in the grocery line, or when you are taking a coffee break?[13]

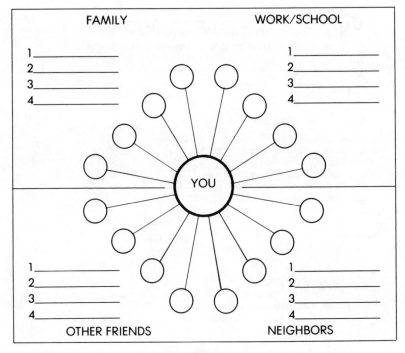

FAMILY

1_____
2_____
3_____
4_____

WORK/SCHOOL

1_____
2_____
3_____
4_____

YOU

1_____
2_____
3_____
4_____
OTHER FRIENDS

1_____
2_____
3_____
4_____
NEIGHBORS

Sociogram

How can we encourage members to invite other persons to church?

1. Use a "sociogram" in your morning worship service as a response to a message on outreach. Emphasize that every person, in every size church, can invite others to church.[14]

As persons fill out the sociogram with specific names, they should be encouraged to keep it with their Bible and *Upper Room* magazine or other devotional guide, and pray daily for those persons. Since all sincere prayer is measured not by our fervent posture during prayer but by our actions afterwards as part of the answer to our prayers, perhaps we will then do what we can to ignite a spark in another person's life and *invite him/her* to an event or service in our church!

WHO DO YOU KNOW . . .
(. . . that could become a member of our church?)

NAME_____PHONE_____

ADDRESS_____ZIP_____

Should join our church because:

_____ Attends Worship Service   REMARKS:_____
_____ Attends Sunday School, Youth   _____
        Group
_____ Attends Men's-Women's Group   _____
_____ In our music program   _____
_____ Attends_____   _____
_____ Survey—Prefers our church
_____ Resident Newcomer   SIGNED_____
_____ Baby on Nursery Roll   YOUR PHONE_____
_____ Baptism, Wedding, Funeral
_____ Was Visited in Hospital   DATE_____
_____ Contributor
_____ Husband/Wife member
_____ Child(ren) in Church School
_____ Other_____

---

2. Use a "Who Do You Know" card in the pew pocket. Again, as a response to a message, periodically use the "Who Do You Know" card to elicit names from the membership of persons who could become part of the fellowship of the church. Ask the members themselves to invite these persons. In addition, the pastor or a visitation team may also visit the persons, or they may receive a telephone contact or be added to the newsletter mailing list.

3. Use bulletin inserts. While on staff of a church in Colorado Springs, a series of bulletin inserts were placed in the Sunday bulletin for a month (it could be once a month), not so much for the information of members but to encourage members to invite their unchurched friends during the week and hand them a reminder about the church. Better yet, the invitation to "Come and See" could be accompanied by an offer to provide transportation for the person.

Come and See . . .

and participate in the ministry of
First United Methodist Church.

EDUCATION — SINGLES

In a 1977 comparative study, First United Methodist Church ranked 7th in church school attendance in United Methodism. First United Methodist Church believes each individual should be significantly involved in a Christian education experience. Therefore:

- There are 20 ongoing adult classes and groups for study and sharing and a wide variety of lay training and personal growth options, including the Bethel Bible Series.

- There are 16 Sunday morning classes for children from nursery through the 6th grade.

- There are Sunday morning and evening classes for youth and Wednesday evening Discipleship studies for both junior and senior high youth.

- Special ministries, such as clown and mime troups, are part of the overall educational experience.

SINGLES

Positive Christian Singles (PCS) is comprised of never married, formerly married and widowed persons age twenty four and onward. Talk It Over (TIO) for singles age 24 and up meets in the church parlor each Sunday evening at 6:00 p.m.

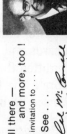

First United Methodist Church
420 N. Nevada Ave.
Colorado Springs, Colorado

Come and See . . .

and participate in the ministry of
First United Methodist Church.

Come and see for yourself

There's **so much** to see at our church !
So much to experience and enjoy !
So many people to share with !
So rich a faith to benefit from !

- If you don't think a large church is capable of being personal — come and see us!

- If you want a Christian program in education designed with a concern for all ages and stages, needs and interests — come and see ours.

- If you like excellence in music with interesting styles and groups — come and hear our 18 music groups.

- If you would like in-depth Biblical studies at whatever stage you happen to find yourself — come and join one of our many groups.

- If you would like to participate in stimulating adult discussion groups with supportive and caring friends — come and participate in one of our 20 adult groups.

- If you are looking for a singles group in your age and interest bracket — come and see what is going on in our church with singles.

- If you want the companionship of other married couples in fellowship, study, or prayer — come and join your marriage with ours.

- If you have a concern for people in our city, or those travelling through, who have emergency needs in housing, clothing, or food — come and see our Social Concern Center.

- If you are interested in Christ's challenge to "go into all the world" — come and see the way we support our missions around the world in education, medical care, agriculture, and community centers.

- If you like preaching with "one foot in the Bible" and the other in the world of practicality — come and hear our preachers.

Yes, it's all there — and more, too !

So accept our invitation to . . .

Come and See . . .

First United Methodist Church
420 N. Nevada Ave.
Colorado Springs, Colorado

4. Use a 3"x5" card that can be filled out in the worship service. Several options are described below that are other variations of cards that can be used to encourage members to invite friends or new residents to church. A complete kit, including bulletin inserts, nametags, posters, and a guide book is available from Discipleship Resources—*Growth Plus: Worship Attendance Crusade Kit*[15]

Invite a friend approach.

Place 3"x5" cards in each church bulletin. If you do not use bulletins, hand a 3"x5" card to each person as he/she enters the church.

At an appropriate place in the worship service, invite each person to take out the card and hold it.

Ask each person to prayerfully consider who among his/her friends, relatives, associates, or neighbors he/she would sincerely want to see as a part of the congregation. Have each person prayerfully write that name on the card.

Ask persons to turn the cards over and as part of their own commitment (if they wish) to sign their own names. This signature is a prayer that God will open a natural opportunity for witness and invitation to the person named. It is also a commitment to use the opportunities that come.

The offering plates are then passed so that the cards can be placed in the plates. They are then brought to the front of the church and dedicated on the altar with a prayer of commitment.

The pastor and/or Committee on Evangelism may wish to go over the cards and periodically give encouragement to those who have committed themselves to contact friends. Rejoice with those who celebrate the fruit of their efforts. Encourage and hold up those who see no outward signs of success.[16]

3"x5" relational evangelism approach.

The plan is based upon the fact that in today's culture most people come to Christ and the church through contacts and invitations from friends, neighbors, or relatives.

Evangelism is built on relationships!

"Andrew . . . first found his brother Simon and he brought him to Jesus."

Matthew gave a great feast and invited many tax collectors.

A Samaritan woman said to other Samaritans: "Come see a man. . . . "

Legion went home to tell his friends and family all that Jesus had done for him.

To implement this plan, take the following steps: Announce the plan one month before "Launch Sunday." (Suggested Launch Sunday is the first Sunday of January or the first Sunday of Lent.) On Launch Sunday distribute 3"x 5" cards to every worshiper. Ask each person to write the names of five persons he or she knows— persons not attending any church. Ask them to pray daily for these persons that they may be won to Christ and the church.

The cards are retained by each worshiper.

Each person holds the card for a prayer of dedication in the worship service. The card is then placed in the person's pocket or purse.

Ask each person to be open to opportunities to share the good news of God's love with these persons in the normal traffic patterns of everyday life (supermarket, work, school, social contact, etc.). Seek to be a special friend to these persons. Seek opportunities to listen truly to them. After listening, say to them, "May I have the privilege of sharing something with you that has enriched my life?" You can share a favorite Bible verse, handwritten on a 3"x 5" card. Examples of these verses could be John 3:16, Acts 2:21, Revelation 3:20.

Invite them to worship with you on Easter—or on a specific Sunday.

If you wish, share your five names with two friends so that there are three praying for five (3 x 5!).

"Again I say to you, if two of you agree on earth about anything they ask, it will be done for them by my Father in heaven" (Matthew 18:19, RSV).

Maintain awareness throughout the congregation of *relational evangelism* by constantly affirming the friendship-relationship potential of each member as each person prays for five others.

On the target Sunday—perhaps Easter or Christmas—distribute 3"x 5" cards to every worshiper again.

This time invite every person to write his or her name on the card with the number that represents that person's worship atten-dance goal for the coming year. In other words, the number "40" would be a goal of 40 Sundays to be present in worship during the coming year. Encourage each person to surpass last year's actual worship attendance average. Many churches will see an increase in worship attendance of at least 10% by allowing persons to set their own personal worship attendance goals.

Worship attendance cards are turned in and dedicated at the al-tar. They are mailed in six months to each person who filled out a card, with a letter celebrating attendance gains and encouraging con-tinued faithfulness (as a total congregation and for individuals).[17]

Andrew card. The card pictured on the following page was used in a church in Forest Lakes, Minnesota. In this instance, a *printed card* was used rather than a blank 3"x5" card. The basic approach to encourage members to invite others is the same.

5. Inaugurate a "Second Sunday Strategy" or Visitor Appre-ciation Sunday.

The Second Sunday Strategy or Visitor Appreciation Sunday sets aside one Sunday a month in a church, such as the second Sunday, especially to invite visitors to church.[18] A small mem-bership church might want to have a Visitor Appreciation Sunday less frequently but still at regular intervals.

On the designated Sunday the worship service is planned with visitors in mind, so that familiar hymns are sung, the sermon addresses needs of those outside the membership, a fellowship time is scheduled following the service, Sunday school classes are alerted to expect visitors during the church school hour, etc. In large membership churches, such a Sunday might include a tour of the building and a chance to meet the church staff at the fellowship gathering following the service. Greeters and ushers should be on the lookout for newcomers on this special Sunday.

When a church has a Second Sunday or Visitor Appreciation Sunday, this emphasis is enhanced when accompanied by the "Come and See" approach or "invite a friend" approach described earlier. If a church uses the "Come and See" bulletin insert on the *first* Sunday of each month, it is logical to have a Visitor Apprecia-tion Sunday the *second* Sunday of each month.

ANDREW CARD

"ANDREW . . . FIRST FOUND HIS BROTHER . . . (AND) BROUGHT HIM
TO JESUS."

John 1:40-42

The purpose of this card is to serve as a reminder that without our personal
invitation our sister, brother, our friend, or neighbor might not hear.

Dear Lord, I lift the following people before you, and pray that, by your
grace, I will have opportunity to bring them, that they might know you.

——————————————— Note: If you would like to ask that a
——————————————— member of the church call on one
——————————————— or more of these persons, jot a note
                            on the other side, about who they
                            are and any information you might
                            have that would be of help to the
                            caller. Then place the card in the
                            offering.

Members must feel free to invite guests *every Sunday*—not
just one Sunday a month! The special strategy adds emphasis to
what is already taking place or sometimes helps a stagnant church
make one concrete step toward increasing the number of first-time
visitors by encouraging the membership to invite others to a special service.

**6. Use a set of questions to stimulate increased awareness of
the need to reach out to others.** Win Arn has developed a series of
questions called "Great Commission Conscience Questions." They
are as follows:

> How do you determine if the leaders/members of a church have a Great
> Commission Conscience? Simple . . . you ask them. Here are ten yes/no
> questions which will give you a clue. Seven of ten affirmative answers are an
> indication of a reasonably strong Great Commission Conscience.
> 1. I see the primary purpose of the church as responding to the Great
>   Commission.
> 2. I have participated in an outreach/training event in the last year.
> 3. I have invited an unchurched friend/relative to a church event in the last
>   six months.
> 4. I would support a motion to designate at least 10% of our budget to
>   outreach events/training/activities to reach our own community with the
>   gospel.

5. I would prefer that the pastor call on non-members more often than members.
6. I would be willing to take a new member/visitor home for dinner at least once every six months.
7. I have intentionally introduced myself to a new member or visitor in the past month.
8. I have talked to an unchurched person about my faith in the past six months.
9. I have prayed for a specific unchurched person in the past month.
10. I would be willing to be the pioneer in a new group or new church fellowship to help reach new people.[19]

VII. Helping Persons Learn to Share Their Faith

Herb Miller, in *Fishing on the Asphalt,* comments: "Someone has estimated that the average church member has listened to 6,000 sermons and 8,000 prayers, sung 20,000 congregational hymns, and asked zero people to accept Christ."[20]

Unfortunately, there is too much truth in Miller's words.

Former President Jimmy Carter was talking about evangelism and faith-sharing to a group of professors of evangelism in seminaries and to other persons involved in evangelism ministries. President Carter related a personal experience which led him to search for new ways to expend his time and energy. He had lost a political election in Georgia and was discouraged about the future. His sister, Ruth, counseled with him and as a result he began, through his denomination (the Southern Baptist Church), to visit in homes of unchurched persons in various states. He kept a record of persons he had influenced positively toward Christ (certainly giving credit to the Holy Spirit in the process). He counted up 140 persons he felt had committed their lives to Christ partially as a result of his efforts. He stated he felt pretty good about that until God seemed to say to him: "Jimmy, you shook 600,000 hands trying to be governor of Georgia and you did that all for yourself. You've only helped 140 persons find salvation in Christ." As I listened to that great but humble man speak, I thought to myself how many pastors or lay persons would worry about *only helping 140 persons find more meaning in their lives through a commitment to Christ!*

How can we help persons learn to share their faith in a nonthreatening, nonmanipulative way with others? First, we must break down the barrier that exists about who an "evangelist" is and enable persons to see that *every Christian* is called to be an evangelist, a proclaimer of God's truth through words and deeds.

Keith Miller, in a workshop some years ago, shared an exercise with the participants that is relevant today.

- Divide persons into pairs and have each person in the group tell of one person, other than immediate family, who had a positive influence upon his/her life and what that person said or did. After several minutes, reverse the sharing so that the second person in each grouping has a chance to share.

- With the group as a whole, ask several persons to share who that person was in *their own life* so that their comments can be summarized in a phrase or few words on newsprint or blackboard.

- Point out to persons that each individual has just been witnessing (not to Christ at this point but to the *positive impact a person has had upon his/her life).*

- Help people to see that such persons as they mentioned were examples of walking incarnate love, which is what an evangelist should be!

- Challenge persons by saying: "You have just been talking about *a person* who has had a positive influence upon your life. Why not go one step further and talk about *the Person, God, and the positive impact that God has had upon your life.* Share something positive about your faith with others in the same conversational way you have been relating to others in this room.

First Peter 3:15 says: "Always be prepared to make a defense to any one who calls you to account for the hope that is in you" (RSV). Ask persons to discuss *why* they are Christians. Use the four Gospels and ask persons to look at the way in which Jesus approached people. Have your Sunday school class or adult discussion group study *Faith-Sharing* by George E. Morris and H. Eddie Fox.[21] Any pastor must find ways to assist his/her parishioners to learn to share their faith naturally and normally. *Effective outreach by a congregation depends upon significant faith-sharing!*

VIII. Outreach through Special Events

Sometimes special events, such as an inspirational speaker, religious-oriented movie or play, mental health seminar, or even a juried art show in the church lounge or fellowship hall sponsored by the fine arts committee, can be an attracting event for newcomers. The Section on Evangelism of the General Board of Discipleship coordinates several revitalization/outreach efforts such as the Lay Witness Mission, Venture in Discipleship, New Life Mission, and Key Event. The Key Event, for example, involves a preparation phase in which the congregation studies *Getting the Story Straight.* A visiting herald then preaches on the four "key events" in the Christian faith—the incarnation (Christmas), crucifixion (Good Friday), resurrection (Easter), and the birth of the Christian church (Pentecost). This phase of the Key Event celebration is "getting the story in." The follow-up to the Key Event involves "getting the story out." Below is the report of a four-point circuit in South Indiana about their Key Event, which they called "Celebrate Christ."

The joint committee began working in the spring and planned the involvement of as many persons and groups as possible so that all would feel a sense of ownership in the mission. Each committee consisted of members of each church who worked side by side throughout the event.

The advance preparation was strengthened by nearly 100 adults attending one of five groups who studied *Getting the Story Straight.* The youth group spent four weeks relating their story to God's story.

The services began with a union service at 10:30 on Sunday morning. . . . On Sunday evening we celebrated Christmas in a church fully decorated for Christmas. On Monday we celebrated Good Friday and the service closed with a service of Communion. On Tuesday, Easter was celebrated and on Wednesday, Pentecost was celebrated. The rotation of the services allowed each church to decorate for their season.

To encourage greater involvement, the children's group and the youth group took turns either singing or acting as hosts, ushers, and greeters. Each service was followed by a fellowship time which included feedback.

RESULTS:

Seven persons made their first-time commitments to Jesus Christ.

Thirty-one persons rededicated their lives to a closer walk with God.

A Charge Men's group was formed and the Women's groups were enhanced.

Two additional small study groups were formed.

Everyone was strengthened by a new sense of community.

Each church felt good about itself since it was able to host an event.[22]

What special event can your church sponsor that might also reach persons outside the congregation with a word of hope or encourage them to visit the church for the first time?

IX. Outreach through the Sunday School

Church Growth, Inc. suggests the following ratios:

- There should be 7 small groups in a church for every 100 members.
- One of every 5 groups that now exist in a church should have been started within the last two years, because groups have a tendency to reach a "saturation point" within 9-18 months after their formation and thus can no longer be effective in incorporating new members.
- Every new member needs to know seven persons well in the first six months to remain active in a congregation.[23]

The above ratios mean that new groups must be started regularly if a church has any hope of reaching out to new persons with the idea of including them in the fellowship as well as membership circle. The Sunday school is a significant means of outreach and inclusion.

Warren Hartman in *Five Audiences* delineates the primary "audiences" which mainline churches reach and can hope to reach in the future. Those audiences and their primary focus are: 1) fellowship group (persons who place a high value on interpersonal relationships), 2) traditionalists, 3) study group, 4) social action group, and 5) multiple interest group.[24]

A church must examine its program offerings to see that the various audiences are addressed. This means that a small membership church with only one adult Sunday school class might start a second class. It means that middle-sized and large membership churches will regularly be starting new classes. Some larger churches use each membership orientation class or inquirers' group as the nucleus of a new class.

In addition to starting new classes, existing adult and youth Sunday school classes should have an evangelism contact person. The duties of such a person might include:

1. Each church school class should have one or more contact persons to relate to the evangelism work area.

2. On cards furnished by the evangelism work area to the

church school department, *in-town* visitors should be indicated. These persons should not just be listed on the card. On the back of each card, there is a place to record the *follow-up of the class* on the visitors to the class. Ideally, in-town visitors would receive a phone call, visit, or note from a class member within a week indicating that the class was delighted to have them as visitors and hope they will attend again.

3. Visits, calls, or notes to class visitors may be made by the evangelism contact person or coordinated by that person. After the follow-up has been made by the class, the reports (perhaps on referral cards) should be placed in the envelope for each class that is returned to the church school department, giving attendance, etc. Reports will be given to the evangelism work area.

4. The evangelism contact person should also report persons who *regularly attend* their particular class that are *non-members* of the church. These persons would not consider themselves visitors to a class.

5. The evangelism work area will keep a prospect file on all visitors to classes that, indeed, are prospects for church membership. Since the classes are "ports of entry" to the church, much contact and nurture must come from the classes themselves. Evangelism should be a concern of every church school class.

Of course, if we are serious about outreach, all new Sunday school classes do not need to be held in our existing facilities. In Gulfport, Mississippi four charges made up of black constituents started an outpost Sunday school in a latchkey housing project. One day these classes may become a new congregation. After surveying 220 housing units, there was a positive response to organizing a Sunday school. On the first day of the outpost Sunday school, 40 persons gathered and were grouped into three classes— children, youth, and adult—led by three teachers and two other workers. The churches came to the people rather than waiting for the people to come to church.

X. Outreach through Children's Ministries

Across the country, Vacation Bible School proves to be the most significant means of outreach to new persons through the small membership church. During a recent summer in Rapid City, South Dakota a church sponsored Backyard Bible Clubs for children.

> The clubs . . . consist of 15 minutes of games, 15 minutes of singing, story telling, and a snack.
> The week prior to meeting, cards are distributed door to door in the neighborhood, inviting the kids.
> The pastors have been handling the leadership role and we now have eight lay persons teaching Clubs, along with the four pastors. We had 97 kids in attendance two weeks ago. More than 90 were from families not affiliated with this church.

While serving a church in a small county seat town in Kentucky some years ago, a woman in the church was loved by all the children and called "Miss Frances." Frances took upon herself the task of coordinating the Mother's Morning Out program and recruited several volunteers to assist. Even in that small town it was not unusual to have two dozen children present to learn from "Miss Frances" or to experience her love for them. Young couples were drawn to the church because of her ministry. "Miss Frances" periodically thought it necessary to paint the basement door to put a fresh coat of paint over numerous handprints. But more important, constant use or even abuse of the building never stood in the way of her ministry to others!

Christ Church in Mobile, Alabama has a significant summer ministry for children with hearing impairment that included in a recent summer:

- **Fantastic Fridays** (Ages Kindergarten-6th grade, 9:30-11:30)
  —Interpreter provided. Activities included the teaching of sign language, the making of beaded Chrismons for the

church, a puppet show, and a visit from the Mobile Police Department to take children's fingerprints and talk to them about being safe children.

- **Sunday 11:00 Church.** An interpreter was provided for Children's Church during this service.

- **Vacation Church School** (August 11-15, 9:00-12:00) Two classes for hearing-impaired children were offered along with other Vacation Church School classes. One class was for younger children (4-7 years old) and the other class was for children 7-10 years old. The classes were taught by a deaf woman and a woman who could hear who knew sign language. The classes included games, Bible stories, and songs, as well as fun and fellowship.

First Church in Collingswood, New Jersey has a marvelous ministry to children with handicapping conditions, even retardation, called "God's Special Kids." The church has a specially equipped van to lift wheelchairs, and an entire area in the education space is set aside for the children. The bulletin boards and murals on the walls *all over the building* proclaim: "God loves children."

Harmony Church in Garland, Texas stresses the importance of children in ways that are meaningful to young parents. For example, when a child is baptized, the couple or parent receives a videotape of the baptism ceremony. Such a permanent record of the event not only is meaningful to the family involved but speaks loudly and clearly to others in the service that the church takes children seriously.

In Charlotte, North Carolina, First Church, a *downtown inner-city church* enhanced its outreach to children by buying a church van and picking up children after school and taking them to choir practice which was held at a *suburban church*. Parents, who were already members or visited the downtown church and wanted to see their children involved, could now see their desires realized by a church that said "we want you"—you do not have to belong to a suburban church to find a significant children's program. Scouts, or other children's programs, can be accommodated in the same manner, by using another facility during the week for special program needs. *"Old First Church" can still reach out to the whole county and every age grouping!*

Other churches have alternative Halloween parties for children or other events that involve many persons and say to the entire community: "This church is here to serve children and you."

XI. Using Special Seasons
of the Church Year

Many church-growth consultants state that Christmas Eve is the number one time in the church year to reach out to unchurched persons. Perhaps because it is a family time and a time when persons think of home and the church more readily, numerous congregations have one or more Christmas Eve services, many including Holy Communion on that special night.

Of course, Lent and the Easter seasons provide opportunities to visibly proclaim the gospel to the community. In New England, a small membership church decided to have a "seed project" during Lent. The project developed in this way:

> Another 'seed project' grew out of a Lenten adult discussion group following Sunday worship. A young high school teacher wanted his church to do something for all people of the community. He suggested that members go to each house in town, give the people a small gift, and invite them to come to worship on Easter Sunday. Someone suggested that the gift be a packet of seeds symbolizing new life. The local hardware store owner agreed to order them. Another person designed and mimeographed a simple folder with a drawing of flowers on the cover. After worship on Palm Sunday, over a dozen adults and children worked side by side coloring in the flowers on the covers and stapling packets of seeds inside next to the message which read: "We want to share these seeds with you in hopes that we, as a community, may grow together. Won't you join us in church on Easter Sunday, or attend the church of your choice?" A brief poem and the schedule of Easter services completed the pages. These folders were delivered to virtually every home in the community (over four hundred). People were surprised and pleased; much goodwill was generated for the church—all because one person identified a need, and people shared their ideas, used their imaginations, encouraged one another, enlisted help, worked together, and did something for someone else.
> That is not a bad model for church programming.[25]

Noonday lunches or breakfasts for business persons during Lent or Advent, short-term Bible studies, outdoor live manger scenes at Christmas, and numerous other happenings provide visibility and new ports of entry for persons into the life of the congregation during special seasons of the year.

XII. Worship as Evangelism

W hat happens in and through the worship service, including what happens in the pulpit, is crucial for the spiritual well-being of persons. See Andy and Sally Langford, *Worship and Evangelism* (Discipleship Resources, 1989). Lawrence Lacour, one-time pastor of First Church in Colorado Springs, has been one of the great communicators in Methodism in recent years. In an article, "How to Put Fire in the Word," Dr. Lacour directs these words to "preachers":

> The primary source of . . . proclamation, of course, is the Bible. No matter how provocative or inspirational the preacher may be, any other message reduces the pulpiteer to the rank of a public speaker.
>
> The Bible reminds us that "God is spirit." We preachers are committed to spiritual subject matter. Chilling the Word, as the *Time* writer described modern preaching ["American Preaching: A Dying Art," *Time*, December 31, 1979 p. 64] is like serving a frozen TV dinner without putting it in the oven. A preacher is expected to be that oven. Is it too much to expect our preaching to be passionate as well as skillful?
>
> Backed by a personal experience of God and personal knowledge of the needs of the congregation, the preacher has listened to the cry of a text. "Preach me!" "Help me do thy work!" The meaning of that text and how it is to accomplish its task in the lives of the congregation becomes the struggle of the week. Alive in the preacher, it must become incarnate in the waiting worshipers. . . .
>
> Your preaching will become passionate in the degree that the gospel and human need are the passions of your life. As you come to your pulpit, you stand between a life-changing gospel and a world that needs changing. Out of your spiritual formation, you can make a difference."[26]

When the gospel has been proclaimed, a chance to respond to the message should be given. No one would prepare a banquet table for friends and then give them no utensils with which to eat. Similarly, by sharing the gospel you call for ways to enter into the abundant life and the way of discipleship spoken about in the message of the service.[27]

Evaluating the music, the liturgy, and every aspect of the

current worship service(s) is important, but sometimes congregations need to consider additional ways to relate to a diverse constituency.

Many churches need to consider having special services to meet the spiritual needs of specific groups—signed services for the hearing impaired, bilingual services or a "language service" in a community where more than one language is spoken. For a church to effectively reach another ethnic or cultural group it may indeed start another worship service in the language of the new residents or people whom the church has overlooked.

In a resort or vacation area, a congregation may do well to offer alternative worship services, such as the "Cowboy Church" mentioned earlier in this volume. For a number of years First Church in Colorado Springs sponsored a summer worship experience called "Church in the Rockies" at the church-owned retreat center about 35 miles from the city. That summer worship experience was attended by some persons who did not have a church home. Eventually, the persons who attended Church in the Rockies became the nucleus of a new congregation.

Most churches will not start outpost worship services or bilingual services, but will rather focus on strengthening their existing services to make them more meaningful to newcomers in the community. A pastor, seeking to be more attuned to needs within the congregation, might ask a series of questions at the close of a Sunday service and urge the congregation to answer those questions in order to help him/her prepare sermons that speak to human hearts and hopes. The pastor could approach the congregation as follows:

> My goal in my preaching is to bring the word of God to the point of your need because I love you and care about you and because I long for you to experience the reality of God's love, wisdom, truth, and power in your life; but I have discovered that just studying Scripture isn't enough. I must also know your concerns, know your needs, know your desires, and here is how you can tell me:
> 1. What is your most urgent question?
> 2. What is your greatest desire?
> 3. What is your greatest need . . . ?[28]

XIII. Outreach through Fellowship-Oriented Events

As Warren Hartman observed in *Five Audiences,* fellowship is a major reason persons seek out the church, if they are searching at all. But more must happen than just encouraging Sunday school classes or other groupings to have a "social event" every month or so. Fellowship should be an intentional factor in outreach to newcomers.

While serving a new congregation in Colorado Springs, the congregation, including visitors, was invited each quarter to participate in round-robin dinners. The dinners were coordinated by a lay volunteer. The round-robin dinners were held the third Friday night of each month. They were for adults, with babysitting provided at a central location or in individual homes as necessary. Each month a couple or single adult served as host/hostess and invited three or four other couples or several single adults to their home. The host provided bread, coffee, or tea and a meat dish for 8-10 people. Another couple/single provided a dessert for 8-10 persons; another, a vegetable; and another, a salad to feed all present.

On the third Friday night perhaps five or six homes were hosting a round-robin dinner, which meant approximately 50 persons were involved in fellowship that night. Each home was encouraged to have present at least one family unit (couple or single) who were not members of the church.

The second month and third month during the quarter, persons rotated to other homes, so that newcomers could know a dozen family units well in the course of a three-month period. The round-robin dinners were planned each quarter of the year. Persons could participate one or more quarters a year or even sign up as a substitute couple/single, to be called if someone could not attend who previously signed up. The only agenda was fellowship. The dinners were a valuable avenue of outreach in the new church.

Serious fellowship may mean simply to encourage church members to invite a person/persons of similar age or interest out to lunch following the worship service on Sunday morning, especially if those persons are visitors in the service. Coffee time before Sunday school or after worship services is an ideal time to welcome newcomers and introduce them to your friends in the church.

Atascocita Church in Humble, Texas sponsored an ice cream social in the early months of the organizational process. The event held in the backyard of a home attracted a number of new persons. Seventy-four persons were present, with 10 families making commitments to join the church.

XIV. Outreach through Direct Mail Advertising

Discovery Church in Richmond, Virginia has depended heavily on direct mail advertising. The pastor, Reverend Jim Lavender, did extensive research in marketing. The church uses repetitive mailings, printed "first class," sent to *names* rather than *occupant!* The pastor helps design the creative advertising pieces which are sent out in the area of the new church. Reverend Lavender has even developed a "Direct Mail Kit" to assist other churches.[29] He feels that the mailings are well worth the $10-15,000 which has been expended on them each year. Although the initial returns are not staggering and are in line with the "law of large numbers" in business mailings, the cumulative effect has been positive for Discovery Church.

Samples of direct mail pieces sent out by Discovery Church and other churches appear on the following pages.[30]

In each case, creative imagination has been used in designing the advertising pieces and they have been "self-contained," i.e., not placed in envelopes.

Mailers need to be realistic about the use of mass mailings. When a mass mailing was sent out with a reply card in a brochure in Sachse, Texas, only 1% of the households returned the card and fewer than that actually joined the congregation in the first few months following the sending of the brochure. Even in that case, however, the pastor felt that the mass mailing did enhance the image of the church in the community, and the publicity piece did serve as one contact among several before persons actually came to the church.

These examples are direct mail pieces which were sent out by congregations.

Does Easter mean beans to your kids?

*If you think you have
to be "religious" to come to church . . .*

It's "Jesus Loves Me."
He still does, you know.

We're a new congregation.
We've been here a year and a half.
And many of our members are back
in church for the first time
in a long while. But they
have found something -- or Someone --
worth getting up for on Sunday mornings.
Come join your neighbors as we
get acquainted again.

ASBURY
◄ THE NEW UNITED METHODIST CHURCH

Do you remember this tune from your childhood?

Je-sus loves me! this I know,

"Do you remember this tune" and "Does Easter mean beans to your kids?" are examples of ads that can be ordered from The Episcopal Ad Project (see endnote 30). "If you think you have to be religious" is a direct mail piece used by St. Luke's United Methodist Church Orlando, FL. Used by permission of James Harnish, pastor.

These slogans were used on successful direct mail brochures from Discovery Church.

All these people have one thing in common. . .

Found A New Beginning in Your new Home

?

Have you ever wanted to hang it up and Start All Over?

XV. Outreach through Senior Citizen Programming

Across the country, increasing numbers of persons are living beyond 65 years of age and the talk of "gray power" is heard more frequently. Thus, it is not only churches in retirement areas such as Florida or Arizona that must do intentional outreach to senior citizens, but churches in every part of the country.

Many churches are sponsoring "Life After Loss" or "Growing Through Loss Conferences" and "Bereavement Support Groups." Many churches offer short-term classes in the church school on "Death and Dying," and the preparations for that inevitable event for every person. Green Valley Community Church in Green Valley, Arizona, lists the following options under its Senior Citizens' Ministry:

Volunteers (office, visitors, etc.)

Knit and Sew group (ours meets every Tuesday throughout the year. Most materials are donated by church members—supply toys, lap robes, sweaters, etc., for missions, agencies)

Interest Groups: Craft groups like Sand Painting, Canvas Backers (embroidery), Quilting, etc.

S.O.S. (Sharing Or Support)—Grief Support Group

Spiritual Growth Retreats (in church facilities or to other locations like Picture Rocks, Holy Trinity Monastery)

Church maintenance and grounds

Bible Study Groups

Couples Club

P.E.P. (People Enjoying People) for singles

Prayer Chain

Book Reviews

Adult Education Classes (for example, the World's Great Religions, Meditation and Health, The Roots of Christianity)

Bowling groups/leagues

Men's group (They sponsor our Food Bank.)

Women's group (Ours has an active Thrift Sale Ladies group. They have one or two large sales each year; now they are doing patio sales in the community.)

Intergenerational activities

Travel together

Tape Ministry (for shut-ins); Radio Broadcast every Sunday morning
Leisure Ministries
Serve as counselors/chaperones for teen groups; share interests, career talks;
   hobbies, etc.
Field Trips
Committee, Board work
Interfaith/Ecumenical work
Serve on the Church Library Committee; Historical Committee[31]

One cutting edge for the church in the future will be adult daycare centers. Because of Alzheimer's disease and other aging processes, many persons who have responsibility for their parents or older adults living in their home find that they need help in coping with the problems of aging. The church can offer tremendous assistance to such concerned persons, as well as to the older adults themselves. (See *It's Your Move* and *It's My Move,* from Discipleship Resources, for further assistance with older adults.)

On the lighter side of older adult ministry, churches are organizing groups such as XYZ Clubs (Extra Years of Zest) or meetings of "Globetrotters," a group that meets periodically to share each other's slides or films of world travel experiences. One pastor even suggested that he was trying to form a RAT Patrol (Retired and Talented). While the name might be questionable, the idea of finding creative and meaningful jobs where senior adults could use their talents is a good idea! "Keenagers" might be a more flattering name. Groups such as these can be ports of entry for older adults into the fellowship circle of any church.

XVI. Outreach through Crisis Support Ministries

Congregations can reach out to hurting persons in numerous ways to help them work through a particularly troublesome crisis. A vital point of contact with many young adults has been *Divorce Recovery Workshops* sponsored by congregations. The curriculum may include Jim Smoke's *Growing Through Divorce, Divorce Recovery Workshop* materials prepared by Discipleship Resources, or other relevant materials.[32]

One new congregation in the West reached out to its community by offering "Getting Well Again" sessions (cancer therapy) led by a retired chaplain. The sessions were open to the entire community. A church in Williamsburg, Virginia provides counseling for families going through bankruptcy and provides guardians for adolescents under house arrest.

Interestingly, sometimes crises offer a chance to meet several needs at the same time. A staff person at Garden Grove Community Church in California explained that they faced a need to establish a "crisis hot-line" service for persons on drugs, threatening suicide, etc. Simultaneously, they realized that a number of senior citizens in a retirement complex not far from the church were looking for a meaningful way to use their time. *The church wisely trained some of the senior citizens to be crisis counselors!*

It should be stated that not all of the persons who are helped in and through crisis situations will unite with the church that has ministered to them. Sometimes the number of persons who actually join a church because the church operates a counseling center, for example, may be very small. *But,* the impact related to outreach is still significant.

I once asked a pastor of a large membership church if he felt many people joined the church he pastored because of its counseling ministry. His reply was revealing: "I do not believe that many of

the persons whom we counsel join our church, but other persons
in our community have joined our church because they know this
is a church that is concerned about people and does such things as
provide a counseling service in our building."

XVII. Outreach through Radio and Television

Many churches have continued to assess the feasibility of outreach through radio and television in a world of video technology. Many pastors and some "experts" question the impact of broadcasting or televising a live worship service. The consensus seems to be that if a church has a significant positive reputation in the larger community, people *will* tune in to the worship service that is broadcast live, or in the case of television, sometimes edited and shown one week later. Some churches edit their hour-long service so that a thirty-minute time slot is filled meaningfully the following week.

Congregations who are contemplating the start-up of a radio or television ministry need to consider the following guidelines:

- A variety of music needs to be included in any broadcast/telecast worship service.
- A worship service should be structured to avoid "dead spots" on the air or television screen. If the worship experience includes prolonged periods of silent prayer or other meditative moments, it may be necessary to edit the service so that it can be broadcast/telecast a week later.
- Leadership in worship services that are being broadcast/telecast need to intentionally include the wider audience outside the sanctuary in the worship experience. Words of greeting to persons listening on the radio or viewing the service on television enhance audience participation. Including those persons in the pastoral prayer or other segments of the service is helpful.
- A broadcast/telecast program should be presented primarily out of concern for other persons. The use of media is a *ministry*.
- In spite of time restrictions and other constraints of the media, a congregation's worship experience should never become a *performance*.

Frazer Memorial Church in Montgomery has perhaps the largest viewing audience, or most widespread audience, in United Methodism because the service is carried nation-wide on cable stations. The pastor, John Ed Mathison, has stated: "I don't know of any ministry that has had the wide-range impact that our television ministry has had in the past three years. We are on numerous cable stations throughout Central Alabama. I receive letters from Selma, Alex City, Sylacauga, Troy, Luverne, Monroeville, and surrounding areas. Last year I had six funerals for people for whom our television ministry became their church during their last days.[33]

Dr. Mathison, speaking of both the radio and television outreach of that church, states:

> God is constantly opening doors in which ministry might be given to people in our area. Radio and television are just two examples. *The best ministry is done people-to-people. More people join Frazer each year because people invite them and bring them to church. The media ministry meets a need in the lives of people, but it can never replace the personal witness of person-to-person.*[34]

Joe Harding was, for many years, senior pastor at Central United Protestant Church in Richland, Washington. For a number of years Joe had thirty-second "spots" on the radio at key traffic times—right before the 7:00 morning news. The radio spots tied in with current musical arrangements and offered a "word of new possibility and hope" to the listeners. Samples of those Growth Plus radio spots, which can be used by local congregations, are available from Discipleship Resources.[35]

Radio and television enhance the efforts of a church already serious about outreach. They can never replace the involvement of each individual in *inviting others* to worship or some other entry point into the community of faith.

XVIII. Outreach through Telemarketing

An expanded version of outreach through the telephone has been developed by Norm Whan, Director of Church Planting, Friends Church Southwest. His program is called "The Phone's for You," and is being used successfully in many areas of the country. Marcus Paul Leaming, pastor of St. James Church in Tulsa, explains the program:

Hi! This is Jim Kerby with St. James Church. We're excited because our church is growing and we'll be moving into our first new building in July. But right now we're calling some of our neighbors to see if we could ask a couple of real quick questions that would help us in putting our programs together. Would that be O.K.?

Yes, I guess so.

Are you actively involved in one of the local churches at this time?

Well—no, we're not.

One of the things that we would like to do if it would be OK . . . We're mailing out a little brochure to the people in our community to tell them about some of the programs that we have available for all age groups. Could we send it to you, just to keep you updated on our progress?

Yes, that would be fine.

Great. You'll be hearing from us in just a couple of days. Thank you very much.

There, in forty-five seconds, is the shot fired across the bow of the unchurched person's life to hopefully begin a long-range relationship of churched with unchurched.[36]

Rev. Leaming goes on to describe the *principles* that will work for telemarketing:

What *are* the principles which will work for telemarketing?

1) The law of large numbers. A percentage of people will respond to an invitation to participate. (Roughly 10% will respond to a new church, 5% to an existing church.) Norm Whan tried it. It worked. Twenty thousand dial-ups produced some two thousand on a mailing list, and over two hundred showed up at a big Sunday celebration. Was it a fluke? Did they get lucky? Another new church tried it. Bingo. Then another. Another—it worked again. Soon over a million calls were made with startlingly similar results.

2) The second principle: if you do A, B, C, and D, the chances are, you'll

produce E. If the format works with a given mix of ingredients, use those in other places. The relationship begun by phone is followed up by correspondence over a five-week period of time: five pieces of mail, another call to the prospects and your big Sunday.

3) The law of large numbers is attainable for a comparatively small number of people. How does it work?

For example:
20,000 calls divided by 4 weeks = 5,000 calls per week
5,000 calls divided by 5 days = 1,000 calls per day
1,000 calls divided by 10 days = 100 dial-ups on each phone per day
100 dial-ups = 2.5 hours × 40 dial-ups per hour.[37]

Since this telemarketing approach is fairly new, several questions still remain to be answered.

If a number of churches of various denominations use the same phone approach in the same area asking the same questions, will hostility eventually be the result? What are the incorporation problems in a congregation when a large number of persons immediately shows up rather than being nurtured or cultivated for membership? When almost the entire group of persons recruited by phone is unchurched, is it difficult to start a church of your *specific denomination?*

As apartment complexes, condominiums, and other real estate developments become more inaccessible to doorstep visits, the phone may be the best approach we have, in spite of any problems associated with it.

Extend Your Welcome

As mentioned in the introduction, no book can be exhaustive in describing factors that impinge upon the internal climate of a congregation or in describing means of intentional outreach in and through a congregation. The book does suggest ideas and stir a person's imagination about what could happen through a congregation as it seeks to relate to its community.

Much more could be said about creative means of outreach through the creation of small groups, such as "Body and Soul" classes for younger women which combine aerobic exercise and Bible study (with nursery provided) or the "Lunch Bunch," a group that gathers with a pastor in the downtown Chicago Loop area, or the Bible studies or fellowship groupings being started in multi-family housing units.[38] In short, much more could be included about any number of subjects or programs of outreach.

This book should cause you to think of one or two things that could work in your church. And, hopefully, it will cause you to want to risk, to become vulnerable, for the sake of persons who need to have a dynamic relationship with God. Programs and events are not ends unto themselves but are worthwhile only if they help persons walk closer with God in their individual and corporate faith journeys. Extend your congregation's welcome.

Endnotes
Part I

1. The letter appeared in *Thrust,* newsletter of the Church of the Servant (United Methodist), Oklahoma City, Oklahoma and is used by permission of the pastor.
2. Ben Johnson, *An Evangelism Primer: Practical Principles for Congregations* (John Knox Press, 1983), 32-33. Used by permission.
3. Herb Miller, *Fishing on the Asphalt* (Bethany Press, 1983), 46. Quoted by permission of Bethany Press.
4. Ibid., 52. Quoted by permission of Bethany Press.
5. *The Unchurched American, 1988.* This scientific study was conducted by the Gallup Organization, Inc., Princeton, New Jersey. Summary statements are used with permission.
6. "Spiritual Health Essential to Growth," *The United Methodist Reporter,* March 15, 1985, Dallas, Texas. Used by permission.
7. "Live Churches—Dead Churches" appeared in the *Frazer Memorial Messenger,* September 30, 1984, and is used with permission.
8. INTELLECT is a trademark of the Artificial Intelligence Corporation. The ad was for IBM software and appeared in the *Wall Street Journal,* April 6, 1984. It is used with permission.
9. John Naisbitt, *Megatrends* (Warner Books, 1982), 39-40.
10. Study done by the Central Illinois Conference, The United Methodist Church.
11. Donald Gerig, "Climate Control: Conditions of a Growing Church," *Leadership,* 1984 Fall Quarter, pp. 40 ff. Copyright 1984 CTi (Christianity Today Publication).
12. "A Modern Parable" was developed for Lands End, a Conference/Retreat Center ministry of the Presbytery of Northern New York, Saranac Lake, New York. Used with permission.
13. Donald Gerig, op. cit., p. 45. Copyright 1984 CTi.
14. Ben Johnson, op. cit., p. 33. Used by permission.
15. Keith Miller, *The Scent of Love* (Word Books, 1983), 199-200.
16. Herb Miller, op. cit., p. 40. Quoted by permission of Bethany Press.
17. "The Faded Purple" sermon was preached by Dr. Joe Pennel at Belmont United Methodist Church, Nashville, Tennessee. Used with permission.

18. William H. Willimon and Robert L. Wilson, *Preaching and Worship in the Small Church* (Abingdon Press, 1980), 42-43.
19. From Kennon L. Callahan, *Twelve Keys to an Effective Church.* Copyright © 1987 by Kennon L. Callahan. Used with permission from Harper & Row, Publishers, Inc., San Francisco, pp. 24-25.
20. Donald Gerig, op. cit., p. 45. Copyright 1984 CTi.
21. Materials for a *Gift Discovery Workshop* developed by Herb Mather and other resources for discovering spiritual gifts are available from Discipleship Resources.
22. Joe Harding, "Strengthening the Local Church," *The Interpreter* (November/December 1978), 17-20.
23. From James D. Anderson and Ezra Earl Jones, *The Management of Ministry.* Copyright © 1978 by James D. Anderson and Ezra Earl Jones. Used with permission from Harper and Row, Publishers, Inc., San Francisco, pp. 172, 172-74.
24. Kennon L. Callahan, op. cit., p. 3.
25. Donald Gerig, op. cit., Copyright 1984 CTi.

Endnotes
Part II

1. Newsletter of Centenary United Methodist Church, St. Louis, Missouri.
2. From Kennon Callahan, *Twelve Keys to an Effective Church.* Copyright 1987 by Kennon L. Callahan. Used with permission from Harper and Row, Publishers, Inc., San Francisco, pp. xxi-xxii.
3. Ben Johnson, *An Evangelism Primer: Practical Principles for Congregations* (John Knox Press, 1983), 41. Used by permission.
4. See James D. Anderson and Ezra Earl Jones, *The Management of Ministry* for a discussion of the primary task of ministry. Copyright 1978 by James D. Anderson and Ezra Earl Jones (Harper & Row).
5. "McDonald's People. Serving customers and the community" © 1988 McDonald's Corporation. Used by permission.
6. Kennon L. Callahan, op. cit., p. 12.
7. Lyle E. Schaller, *Assimilating New Members* (Abingdon, 1978), 22, 23, 24.

8. *Frazer Memorial Messenger,* March 29, 1987. Frazer Memorial United Methodist Church, Montgomery, Alabama.

9. W. James Cowell, *Sponsoring New Congregations* (Discipleship Resources, 1985). This is a motivation booklet to encourage existing churches to sponsor new congregations.

10. Kirk McNeill, *Start-Up Manual for New Sunday Schools* (Discipleship Resources, 1985). This manual is also available in Spanish.

11. Suzanne G. Braden, *Evangelism Ministries: Planning Handbook* (Discipleship Resources, 1987).

12. *The Unchurched American, 1988.* This scientific study was conducted by the Gallup Organization, Inc., Princeton, New Jersey. Summary statements are used with permission.

13. *Frazer Memorial Messenger,* December 2, 1984. Frazer Memorial United Methodist Church, Montgomery, Alabama.

14. Sociogram from Ronald K. Crandall and L. Ray Sells, *There's New Life in the Small Congregation* (Discipleship Resources, 1983).

15. A manual, *Growth Plus: The Vision,* by Joe A. Harding is available from Discipleship Resources for churches interested in commitment to growth.

16. I am indebted to Herb Mather, Assistant General Secretary, Section on Stewardship, General Board of Discipleship for the "Invite a Friend" approach used in this book.

17. I am indebted to Joe A. Harding of the Section on Evangelism for the 3 x 5 relational evangelism approach described in this book.

18. A brochure, "Second Sunday Outreach," is available from Discipleship Resources, Nashville, Tennessee. Free.

19. "Great Commission Conscience Questions" used by permission of Win Arn, Church Growth, Monrovia, California.

20. Herb Miller, *Fishing on the Asphalt* (Bethany Press, 1983), 158. Quoted by permission of Bethany Press.

21. H. Eddie Fox and George E. Morris, *Faith-Sharing: Dynamic Christian Witnessing by Invitation* (Discipleship Resources, 1986). This book contains questions for reflection and action at the end of each chapter.

22. This report is from the Monroe City charge of the South Indiana Conference. For more information on the New Life Mission, Key Event, or New World Mission, address: Director of Preaching Evangelism, General Board of Discipleship, P. O. Box 840, Nashville, TN 37202.

23. Ratios from Church Growth, Inc., Monrovia, California. Used by permission.

24. Warren J. Hartman, *Five Audiences* (Abingdon, 1987).

25. From Jeffery S. Atwater, "Programming in Small Congregations: Factors Which Aid or Limit," *Small Churches Are Beautiful,* edited by Jackson W. Carroll. Copyright 1977 by the Hartford Seminary Foundation. Used

with permission from Harper and Row, Publishers, Inc., San Francisco, pp. 122-23.

26. Lawrence L. Lacour, "How to Put Fire in the Word," *Circuit Rider* (May 1984). The United Methodist Publishing House. Used by permission.

27. A helpful resource is *Invite: What to Do after the Sermon* by O. Dean Martin (Discipleship Resources, 1987).

28. Questions are used by permission of Bob Orr, Church Growth, Inc., Monrovia, California.

29. The *Direct Mail Kit for Churches,* copyright 1987 by James E. Lavender, Jr., can be ordered from 2627 Pleasant Run Drive, Richmond, VA 23233.

30. The Episcopal Ad Project provides ads for many different denominations, such as the ads used by Asbury United Methodist Church in Birmingham, Alabama. Contact: The Episcopal Ad Project, 4201 Sheridan Avenue, South, Minneapolis, MN 55410.

31. I am indebted to Madonna Moess, Diaconal Minister, Green Valley Community Church, Green Valley, AZ.

32. *Divorce Recovery Workshop: Leader's Guide and Participant's Guide* by Doug Morphis are available from Discipleship Resources, Nashville, Tennessee.

33. *Frazer Memorial Messenger,* March 2, 1986. Frazer Memorial United Methodist Church, Montgomery, Alabama.

34. *Frazer Memorial Messenger,* February 23, 1986. Frazer Memorial United Methodist Church, Montgomery, Alabama.

35. *Growth Plus: Radio Spots Audio Cassettes* produced by Joe Harding (Discipleship Resources, Nashville, Tennessee).

36. Marcus Paul Leaming, "Telemarketing: A Tool or a Toy for the Church," *New Congregational Development* Newsletter, Volume 4, Number 3 (General Board of Discipleship). This article also appeared in *Forward,* the journal of the Foundation for Evangelism, Lake Junaluska, North Carolina, and is used with permission.

37. Ibid.

38. A helpful resource for outreach to multi-family dwellings is David Beal, *Opening Doors to Multi-Family Housing* (Metropolitan Missions Department, Home Mission Board, Southern Baptist Convention, Atlanta, GA).